WEST WITH THE LIGHT

MY LIFE IN NATURE

For Annabelle

Brian Jackman

WEST WITH THE LIGHT

MY LIFE IN NATURE

First published in the UK in August 2021

Bradt Guides Ltd
31a High Street, Chesham, Buckinghamshire, HP5 1BW, England
www.bradtguides.com

Print edition published in the USA by The Globe Pequot Press Inc,
PO Box 480, Guilford, Connecticut 06437-0480

Text copyright © 2021 Brian Jackman
Photographs copyright © 2021 Brian Jackman and individual photographers
(see below)
Edited by Rachel Fielding
Cover design and illustration by Jasmine Parker
Layout and typesetting by Ian Spick, Bradt Guides
Production managed by Sue Cooper

ISBN: 9781784778361

British Library Cataloguing in Publication Data
A catalogue record for this book is available from the British Library

Photographs of George Adamson reproduced by kind permission of
Tony Fitzjohn

Printed by Zenith in the UK
Digital conversion by www.dataworks.co.in

ABOUT THE AUTHOR

Brian Jackman is an award-winning journalist and author with a lifelong passion for travel and wildlife. Although his travels have taken him around the world he is best known as Britain's foremost writer on African wildlife safaris and has spent more than three years in total under canvas in the bush. His books - all published by Bradt - include *Wild About Britain*, *Savannah Diaries* and *The Marsh Lions* (written with Jonathan Scott and acclaimed as an African wildlife classic). He is also a Fellow of the Royal Geographical Society, a trustee of the George Adamson Wildlife Preservation Trust and an ambassador of Tusk Trust.

CONTENTS

PART ONE

SUNSHINE AND SHADOWS

'Streamline train, fastest train around,
Hardworking stranger, you ain't gonna get me down,
I'm gonna leave in the morning,
Baby on that streamline train.'

The Vipers Skiffle Group

CHAPTER ONE

IN November 1936 I was one of more than 100,000 people who flocked to Sydenham to watch the Crystal Palace burn down. Built for the Great Exhibition of 1851, this mighty showpiece of the Victorian Age was designed by Sir Joseph Paxton and originally stood in what is now Kensington Palace Gardens. Three years later its 990,000 square feet of plate glass were dismantled and rebuilt on Penge Common. Nobody will ever know what started the blaze, but it became one of the biggest fires London had ever seen, the flames from its blackened cast-iron carcass lighting up the night sky in a glow that was visible across eight counties.

The fact that I have no recollection of this historic event is because I was only one year old at the time and was wheeled there in my pram by my mother from her family home in West Norwood. In later years she loved to tell me how she had been accosted by an elderly lady who stared at my white woollen baby clothes in amazement before declaring in a shrill cockney voice: 'Oh my Gawd – ain't 'e clean!'

At least I can remember the house where my mother grew up in Gipsy Road, a typical Victorian semi built of yellow London stock bricks with bay windows and a basement separated by iron railings from the street outside. Here lived my Grandad, Frederick Grant, who had been a Royal Marine, and my Nan, Agnes, an apple-cheeked country girl from Potton in Bedfordshire. Although he had lived in England all his life, I was immensely proud that my

Grandad bore the name of an illustrious Highland clan and have always felt a closeness to Scotland and all things Scottish I can never quite explain.

Although the house itself was always spotless the garden was little more than a grimy backyard whose bare earth was the domain of a pet tortoise that once chased me, or so I complained, thus becoming the cause of much mirth in later life.

I adored Grandad Grant, who could tap out the tune of a hornpipe on his cheeks and always made a fuss of me. He was incredibly knowledgeable and would regale me with stories about the Sioux and other Native American tribes. During the Great War he had fought in the trenches until he was gassed. For the rest of his life, he had weak lungs and no sense of smell, but at least he had come home to his family.

My mother Lilian – Lil to everyone who knew her – was the eldest of his four children, the others being my Auntie Violet and Auntie Winnie and my Uncle Fred. Violet (always known as Vi) was my favourite aunt, with a zest for life and a tremendous sense of humour. She was married to my Uncle George, a big, genial, freckled man with a deep voice and a luxuriant ginger moustache who had a successful career in the chemical industry. For a time, they lived at Potters Bar, where I have vague recollections of gathering bulrushes from a pond on a golf course at the bottom of their garden. Later, when my Cousin Jennifer, their only daughter, was still a toddler, they moved to a rather grand detached house in Darley Dale, near Matlock in Derbyshire.

Uncle Fred was married to Auntie Maimie, and although their son Peter was two years younger than me, he became my inseparable companion. When he was still a toddler, his parents divorced. Fred won custody and took Peter to live with him in Shirley, not far from Crystal Palace, where my Nan had also moved after Grandad Grant had died.

I remember Uncle Fred treating the entire family to dinner at the Trocadero Restaurant in London's West End. It must have been in the austerity years just after the Second World War, and I was given an incomprehensible menu from which I chose a chicken curry, much against the advice of my parents, and found it to be utterly delicious. Later, when Fred married my Auntie Pam and moved into a flat above a parade of shops in Thornton Heath, Cousin Peter and I spent many happy times with them, playing canasta or shove ha'penny, or impromptu games of skill, such as trying to hit a pebble with a bouncing tennis ball in the backyard. Pam was much younger than Fred, a buxom girl with dark brown eyes and a love of opera and travel. Together they went to music festivals in Ireland and enjoyed cultural holidays in Paris.

As for my Auntie Win, she was married to Uncle Alec who was a fireman and died in the Blitz. I am sorry to say I can hardly remember him, even though he generously built me a beautiful wooden toy train, painted bright red and big enough to sit on. Win eventually remarried towards the end of the war – this time to my Uncle Vic, a Canadian commando who was wounded in the Dieppe Raid – and went off to live with him in the Canadian backwoods. When I asked him how many Germans he had killed, his cheerful personality changed. 'Brian,' he said in a sombre voice, 'we just don't talk about those things.'

For reasons I never really understood, we were always much closer to my mother's family. The exception was my father's brother, Uncle Maurice, who married my Auntie Beattie and lived in Reigate in a typical 1930s semi with a row of Scots pines in their garden. As theirs was a childless marriage I often stayed with them and was treated like the son they never had.

I also had another Auntie Win. This was Auntie Winifred Luchford – not a real aunt but a close friend of my mother who became my godmother and used to take us for pre-war drives into the Sussex countryside in her Morris Eight two-door saloon car.

On one trip we stopped for a picnic beside a bridge over the River Eden. It must have been in May, because although I cannot have been more than four years old, I can clearly remember water meadows thick with buttercups, and the momentary wave of vertigo I experienced when my father lifted me up to peer over the parapet at the swarms of tadpoles in the water below.

My mother went to a school in Gipsy Hill where she won several book prizes for her English essays. On leaving school she worked as a secretary and typist, and her big blue eyes attracted many admirers. Among them was my father, Stanley, one of seven brothers who lived not far away at No. 39 Auckland Hill and belonged to one of the 480 Jackman families registered as living in London at the turn of the century.

My father was an accomplished amateur footballer, a stocky right-winger with bandy legs and a good turn of speed, who played for Wimbledon in the Isthmian League. With his coal-black hair and trim moustache he stole my mother's heart away and the boy she had been courting, a poet known to my father and his cronies as 'Cissy' Shay, posted her a lament in which each verse ended with the line, 'Oh faithless Lily Grant.'

Like many young men of his generation, he had all his teeth extracted on his 21st birthday, but it made no difference to their blossoming romance. Nor did his fondness for smoking a pipe. So, dentures and Three Nuns tobacco regardless, they were soon engaged, although it would be another seven years before their wedding in 1933.

This was because my mother had insisted that they should not get married until they could afford to spread their wings and move out to the newly fashionable Surrey suburbs.

Theirs had been an Edwardian London I can still dimly remember, a gas-lit world of sulphurous fogs and reeking chimneys, of clanging trams and cobbled streets that echoed to the clip-clop of horse-drawn bakers' vans and the sing-song street cries of rag-and-bone merchants.

Nothing summed up that bygone age more vividly than my father's home on Auckland Hill, a gaunt red-brick house, three storeys high, with a monkey puzzle tree in the back garden, overlooking the cutting in which electric trains rattled past on their way to Victoria station.

Inside on the ground floor was a scullery with a shallow china sink, and steps leading upstairs into the old-fashioned living room in which we always sat down to tea. In addition to his footballing skills my father was also a competent amateur oil painter, and in one corner hung one of his pictures, a portrait of an Airedale Terrier that had once been a family pet.

Dominating the room was an ornate cast-iron fireplace, polished with black lead and surrounded by a brass fender richly upholstered with green leather seats, and at its centre stood a table covered in a baize cloth on which sat a handsome green parrot in a big brass cage.

Sadly, I never knew Grandad Jackman. He had run a successful laundry business until he died in the same year that I was born; but

Granny Jackman was still very much alive, and her shrill voice filled the room. 'Hello, Stanley,' she would cry as she welcomed my father on our arrival, at which point her words would be expertly mimicked by the parrot. 'Hello, Stanley,' it would shriek, time and again until in the end she would whack the bars of the cage with a bamboo cane before throwing a cloth over it. Only then, once peace was restored, and with no other sound but the chimes of a grandfather clock somewhere deep in the bowels of the house, would tea be served, with chocolate wafers from the wooden biscuit barrel that shared the place of honour on the table with the parrot.

But I am jumping the gun. After my parents' marriage and their honeymoon at Minehead in Somerset, they had acquired enough capital to take out a mortgage on No. 34 Briarwood Road in Stoneleigh, one of the many hundreds of newly built semi-detached houses spilling across the fields between the London Road and the Southern electric railway line on its way south to Epsom. During the reign of Henry VIII this long-vanished sweep of Surrey farmland had been part of the Great Park of Nonsuch Palace but was sold off in the late 17th century and was fast becoming part of suburbia.

Ironically, in view of Stoneleigh's link with King Henry, most of the houses were built in the Tudorbethan or mock Tudor style that manifested itself in a pastiche of half-timbered gables and diamond-paned windows – a mirror image of the development taking place on the other side of London, where the Metropolitan Railway (later the Metropolitan tube line) had extended its tentacles northwards from Baker Street to Aylesbury and Amersham, creating the classic suburbs that would later become known as Metroland.

Stoneleigh's newly constructed station enabled my father to commute to Waterloo where he worked as a clerk for the Southern

Railway, totting up endless columns of figures in a Dickensian office. It was not the most exciting of occupations but at least he was bringing home a salary. 'Get a job, any job,' my grandfather had urged him, because work was hard to come by in the aftermath of the Great Depression.

His reward came in 1933, by which time my parents had saved enough to obtain a mortgage and realise their dream of swapping London's grimy streets for a new life in the leafy suburbs; and in April 1935, two years after my parents had moved into Briarwood Road, I was born in Epsom Hospital.

Sadly, what should have been a time of hope and fulfilment was overshadowed by the events hanging over Europe. That same year saw Mussolini's Italy invade Ethiopia, an ominous sign of the rise of fascism, and in Germany, having swept to power only two years earlier, Hitler was busily creating the Luftwaffe whose warplanes would have a profound change on my life.

Nevertheless, my earliest childhood memories were filled with sunshine and here I grew up, wrapped in an orderly world that moved to its own quiet rhythms, genteel and secure, smelling of lilac bushes and creosote fences, comforted by the weekend purr of lawnmowers, like the breathing of a heavy sleeper, and the clackety-clack of distant wheels as the electric trains rushed by.

In recent decades, suburbia has become widely derided for the lifestyle it represents: a place where too much smugness lurks, where materialism is venerated and the art of keeping up with the neighbours has been honed to the finest edge of subtlety. But the old values – security, tolerance, a respect for privacy and tidiness – endure. For all their faults, the suburbs are strongholds of moderation whose inhabitants can raise their families free from the worst excesses of ugliness and inner-city blight. Suburbia may be a mongrel, neither true megalopolis nor full-blown countryside; but my parents were happy there and so was I.

What its critics forget is this vast monument to the 1930s was built by the dreams of ordinary folk like my parents whose deepest wish was a fresh start and a home away from London, and it was the railways that made their great escape possible.

So out from London's grimy epicentre flowed the red-brick tide of new estates, its ripples of pebble-dash and mock Tudor gables lapping ever deeper into rural Surrey; and the rail tracks flowed with it, the names of their stations intoned like a litany over platform loudspeakers: Raynes Park, Motspur Park, Worcester Park, Stoneleigh…

Suddenly, the brave new world was only half an hour away down the line from London. No longer was it necessary to live close to where you worked. You could spend all day at your desk in the City and still be home in time for tea, looking out at your suburban back garden with its lupins and pear trees and crazy paving. It was a marvellous freedom, even if the price paid was a life of thraldom as a railway commuter.

CHAPTER TWO

MY parents were typical of the newlyweds forging a bold new lifestyle on this outermost frontier of the South London suburbs. When they first moved into Briarwood Road there were cowslips at the bottom of the garden, and pheasants still came rocketing over the lawn from adjacent meadows not yet built on.

By the time I arrived, the tide's edge of commuter-land had rolled even further south, leaving us marooned in a sea of rooftops in which the parameters of my infant world were defined by the Broadway shopping parade at one end of the road and Nonsuch Park at the other.

It was by learning the names of the Broadway shopfronts (Woolworths, Payantake, Frost's the Corner Shop) that I was able to read long before I was five years old. My favourite was the Co-op, an old-fashioned grocer's, in which cash and receipts were transferred by means of overhead wires that whizzed back and forth from a counting house at the back.

As a source of wonder it was surpassed only by the X-ray machine that stood outside the shoe shop. Here, if you pushed your shoes into the space at the bottom, you could see all the bones of your feet silhouetted against a ghostly green background. It was later removed after discovering that the X-rays posed a serious health risk.

Nonsuch, on the other hand, was a haven of solitude. Separated from the rest of suburbia by a ditch and a long wooden fence, it lay between Ewell and North Cheam, on the opposite side of the

A24 – the London Road – along which crowds of racegoers hurried down to Epsom on Derby Day.

Behind the fence stood a line of trees whose dappled glades were alive in summer with speckled wood butterflies, and although Nonsuch was called a park it was more like an island of rolling farmland, its meadows enclosed by hawthorn hedgerows and sluggish ditches full of newts.

Within its confines stood an elegant mansion built in the late 18th century and revamped in 1806 like a vision of Henry VIII's lost palace. Its walled gardens were a delight, with rose trellises and gravel walks surrounding a grassy dell that had once been a chalk pit, but it was the woods and fields of the park itself that would become my childhood playground.

Linking the park and the Broadway was Briarwood itself, its roadside verges bright with almond blossom, its pavements bordered by neat front gardens whose privet hedges and gates with spokes like setting suns provided the perfect setting for a John Betjeman idyll of bay-windowed semis with pebble-dash walls and front doors adorned with stained-glass images of lighthouses and galleons in Art Deco style.

Here at No. 34, my childhood unfolded in the long ago when house sparrows chirruped from every rooftop and bread was delivered by horse-drawn van from the baker's shop in Ewell High Street.

Every morning after breakfast the dads would set off with their brollies and trilbies to catch the 8.15 to Waterloo. The next exodus was the schoolkids, the boys in uniform caps and blazers, the girls in tunics with bobbing pigtails, leaving the mums free to wrestle with the Monday washing while I was left to my own devices.

Like everyone's garden in Briarwood Road, ours was a modest, fenced-in rectangle measuring no more than a hundred feet long, with a wooden shed and a vegetable patch reached by a concrete path.

Here my father grew King Edward potatoes and erected bamboo wigwams for his runner beans, while beside the path lay flower beds where snapdragons and wallflowers – my mother's favourites – blossomed between clumps of golden rod. A Victoria plum and two Cox's apple trees provided shade as well as fruit, and in front of the kitchen was a lawn on which I played for hours, hiding my toy soldiers in the hollows and crevices under the path's concrete edges.

One fine sunny morning, out in the garden with the kitchen windows opened wide, I heard for the first time a sound that stopped me in my tracks like a hypnotised rabbit. It was a Scottish pipe band playing 'The Flowers of the Forest' on the wireless, and even now whenever I hear that haunting lament, I feel the hairs rising on the back of my neck, as if confirming the existence of the Clan Grant genes in my blood.

In summer, confined to my cot for an afternoon rest, I watched next door's poplars trembling in the breeze, casting their dappled light across the bedroom ceiling while the cumulus clouds piled into the sky above them, their shape-shifting profiles assuming the stern faces of imaginary giants.

Downstairs in the front room stood a rosewood bookcase containing a complete set of *Children's Encyclopaedias* and other books won by my mother as school essay prizes. Among them was a history of Britain called *Little Treasure Island, Her Story and Her Glory* by Arthur Mee, a collection of Irish folk tales with illustrations by Arthur Rackham, and *My Book of Beautiful Legends*, a particular favourite of mine with St George and the Dragon on the cover.

Avidly, I devoured the tales of Beowulf and King Arthur, Ulysses, Jason and the Golden Fleece; and being fair-haired, my heroes were always the Anglo-Saxon underdogs such as Robin Hood and Hereward the Wake, waging guerrilla war from Sherwood Forest and the Lincolnshire Fens against the Norman invaders.

I must have spent hours with my nose in a book, sprawled on the settee with the afternoon sunlight streaming in through the windows; but winter was the time when being indoors came into its own. No central heating existed for us in those far-off days before global warming. From November onwards it was normal to wake up and find frost patterns engraved on the inside of the windows; and whenever the temperature fell well below zero my father would have to climb into the loft with a blowlamp to thaw frozen pipes.

In winter, the kitchen was the only warm room in the house, yet even there, icicles clung to the bottoms of the windows where condensation had run down the panes and frozen solid after the stove had gone out, and my father's first task of the day was to refill it with coke and ignite it with a gas lighter. Once alight, it created a cocoon of comfort in which we huddled at breakfast time, sharing its confined space with Jimmy, a pedigree wire-haired fox terrier, and Simon, a ginger tomcat.

Breakfast itself was either a boiled egg with buttered toast cut up into 'soldiers', or a bowl of Fru-Grains, a long-vanished breakfast cereal which looked like bits of rusty shrapnel but was addictively delicious. Afterwards I would set out my pencil box on the kitchen table and draw pictures of dinosaurs on the bloodstained white paper used to wrap meat from the butcher's shop in the Broadway.

Like many small boys I was clearly fascinated by prehistoric animals, as evidenced by this extract from a letter written in pencil to my Aunt Vi in 1942, in which I have retained the spelling mistakes and punctuation from the original.

At dawn in the history before man came there were
huge animals and bird and fish there were the
mammoth the sabre-tiger and the pteradactril the
trigartops the Dipladocus and the ichthyosouros. The
Dipladocus had a backbone of 90 feet. The end.

Lunch was usually the main meal of the day, heated up for my father when he came home from work. My mother's cooking was plain and simple and thoroughly English, untainted by garlic, olive oil or anything dismissed by my father as 'that foreign muck', but none the worse for that. In fact, the dishes she lovingly provided were delicious: stuffed hearts, rabbit stew with dumplings, boiled cod with mashed potatoes and parsley sauce followed by apple pie for afters. I even enjoyed the cold meat leftovers from Sunday's roast lunch that always turned up on Mondays embellished with home-made pickled onions.

Then came the best part of the day, especially in winter when the dining room curtains were drawn and the fire was lit in time for five o'clock tea (Lyle's Golden Syrup sandwiches or cheese on toast), eaten on a tray while listening to *Children's Hour*. This programme was so popular that by 1939 it had an audience of four million. It was always introduced by Uncle Mac – Derek McCulloch – who was head of children's broadcasting from 1933 to 1951 and who ended every programme with the familiar phrase, 'Goodnight children, everywhere.'

His was also the voice of Larry the Lamb, one of *Children's Hour's* best-loved characters who appeared in *Toytown*, together with Dennis the Dachshund and Mr. Growser. Other regulars included Norman and Henry Bones, the boy detectives, and a countryside programme called *Out with Romany*.

Dull indeed would have been those winter evenings had it not been for our Bakelite wireless set with its sunburst design. Being allowed to stay up late to listen to *Monday Night at Eight* was a special treat when, huddled ever closer to the fire as the wind moaned and the temperature dropped outside the French windows, I would stare into the embers, imagining dragons and monsters in the glowing caves between the coals while my father baked potatoes in the hot ashes under the grate.

Opposite the windows was a cupboard under the stairs in which all my toys were kept, and in which I was sometimes shut up as a punishment for bad behaviour. As a small boy I was so afraid of the dark that at bedtime I begged my parents to leave the hall light on so I could see its comforting glow shining under my bedroom door. No wonder I hated being locked in the toy cupboard – until one day it suddenly dawned on me that there was still enough daylight coming under the door for me to amuse myself. When at last my mother came to let me out, she found me playing happily with my Meccano set and the threat of incarceration in the toy cupboard was abandoned.

But far greater horrors awaited, and none worse than visits to the dentist. The surgery's antiseptic smell was enough to give me the shivers, and fillings were the stuff of nightmares. Using an archaic combination of wheels and pulleys, the dentist's drill was powered by a treadle and employed with all the finesse of a garage mechanic's angle grinder.

Even now I find it hard to imagine which was worse – the sickly odour of the chloroform pad being pressed over my face before an extraction or the grinding pain of a tooth being filled. Both, I suspect, were the penalty for eating too many sandwiches spread with Lyle's Golden Syrup, extracted by the spoonful from its distinctive green and yellow tin adorned with a sleeping lion and the quotation: 'Out of the Strong Came Forth Sweetness'.

The same vile anaesthetic was used when my tonsils were removed at St. Anthony's Hospital in North Cheam. In those days it was run by the Daughters of the Cross of Liège, a pious coven of stone-faced nuns whose devotion appeared to fall short of offering kindness and compassion to a frightened three-year-old. Even the homemade lemonade my mother had left me was confiscated, and I can still remember the operating theatre whose glass cabinets, gleaming with shiny metal kidney dishes and sinister-looking surgical tools, filled me with dread until, struggling to evade the vile-smelling chloroform pad, I was put to sleep.

The only consolation occurred after the operation when I was given ice cubes to suck to ease my sore throat – a great novelty in the 1930s when my parents could not afford a fridge. I was told much later I had made such a fuss – crying for hours on end – that in desperation the nuns sent for my mother and begged her to take me home.

Despite these tribulations my overall memory of those early years is one of deep contentment. Having grown up it is easy to forget one's perspective of life experienced at kneecap level; but if I cast my mind back, I can still conjure up how it was in those idyllic pre-war summers, when I rode up and down the pavement on my tricycle, or my mother would make us a picnic of hard-boiled egg or Shippam's Fish Paste sandwiches and wade out into the unshorn fields of Nonsuch.

There, sprawled on a rug at my mother's feet, was a different world. 'Do you like butter?' she would ask, holding a buttercup under my chin so that its golden colour glowed on my skin.

To my infant eyes those childhood meadows were a jungle, a forest of tall stems fizzing with grasshoppers. Small butterflies flipped overhead, bluer than the sky itself, and from somewhere above and beyond the nodding foxtails wood pigeons cooed with husky voices, as drowsy as the day itself.

When Grandad Grant came to stay, he would also take me to the park and hide biscuits in hollow trees, telling me they were caches of pemmican left by a hunting party of Sioux warriors; and afterwards, when I had found and eaten the biscuits, he would whoop and holler his way through an Indian war dance until his war-ravaged lungs got the better of him.

I loved my grandad more than I can say. In those first years of my life, he was my best friend, but all too soon his visits to Briarwood grew more infrequent until the day I was taken to see him in hospital. He was terminally ill with cancer of the bladder, a shadow of himself, washed up like flotsam against his pillows. Without understanding his condition, I must have fidgeted as we sat with him. 'Don't jog the bed,' he said harshly, in a tone I had never heard him use before. They were the last words I ever heard him say.

CHAPTER THREE

LITTLE did I know it, but my early childhood, like the decade itself, was coming to an end as Hitler's storm troopers goose-stepped into Poland. Two days later, at 9am on 3rd September 1939, Britain and France gave Nazi Germany an ultimatum: withdraw from Poland or face the consequences. No such promise was received and by lunchtime we were at war.

My first introduction to the Blitz took place one afternoon in the autumn of 1940. We had gone into the front garden, having heard aircraft approaching, and were innocently watching a squadron of heavy bombers passing high overhead in close formation. Suddenly the air-raid sirens began to wail, and our next-door neighbour said, 'Oh my God, they're German!'

Hurriedly, we retreated indoors, where my mother surrounded me with a pile of cushions. Moments later we heard the dull crump of not-too-distant explosions, and afterwards, when my father came home from work, we discovered that the raiders had been intercepted by the RAF and jettisoned their bombs over Tolworth before turning tail.

At the age of five I joined Stoneleigh East Infant School in Sparrow Farm Road where, under the authoritarian gaze of Miss Brickwood, the head teacher, I learned to write, using chalk and a slate tablet. The classrooms smelt of milk – every child was given a third-of-a-pint bottle every morning. School dinners were also provided, but the over-boiled vegetables were so revolting that my mother always made me a packed lunch instead.

At playtime I was immediately initiated into the arcane world of playground lore, reciting the same scraps of meaningless doggerel that must have been handed down for generations: *'Eeny meeny macka racka, rare eye dominacka, chicka bocka lolly poppa om-pom-push.'*

When choosing teams for playground games we would stand in a circle with both fists extended, chanting:

> *One potato, two potatoes, three potatoes, four,*
> *Five potatoes, six potatoes, seven potatoes, more.*

While this was happening, one of us would go around tapping each fist in turn. Whoever's fist was tapped when the rhyme ended had to put it behind his back, whereupon the chant began again until only one fist was left in the circle – that of the boy who was then chosen to be 'it'.

When the sirens moaned, we filed out of class and into the air-raid shelters dug in the playing field, to sing 'Run Rabbit Run' while the Luftwaffe roared overhead to drop their bombs on London.

All too soon the bombing raids became commonplace. So did the dogfights I sometimes witnessed as the Spitfires and Hurricanes of Fighter Command took on the might of the Luftwaffe.

By day, the skies were filled with barrage balloons that floated high above the rooftops like obscenely swollen silver fish. At night, the air-raid sirens howled their warning, followed by the thump of exploding shells as the artillery batteries guarding London loosed off a hail of ack-ack (anti-aircraft gunfire) at the approaching enemy squadrons and searchlights raked the darkness.

As the war progressed, everyone, including children, was issued with gas masks. Windows were covered with tape to prevent injuries from flying glass, and air raid wardens wearing tin hats and wellington boots patrolled the streets, shouting 'put that light out' if anyone failed to draw their blackout curtains in time.

Although London was the prime target, some bombs also fell on our quiet streets. Sometimes, when walking to school in the mornings, I would pass the smoking ruins of a neat mock Tudor semi which had been hit in the night, its roof blown off, ceilings down and wallpapered bedrooms indecently exposed to the public gaze. Often there were treasures to be gleaned from the previous night's raids in the form of shrapnel, whose bright fragments of jagged metal littered the roads. If you were lucky you might pick up the brass nose of an anti-aircraft shell or – the most sought-after trophies of all – the shiny fins of an incendiary bomb.

What dark days these must have been for my parents. Being over 40, my father was deemed too old to fight and joined the Home Guard instead, where he learned how to fire a .303 rifle, construct booby traps, destroy tanks and survive in the open if the Germans ever managed to invade us. Otherwise, there was little he could do except follow the official mantra of the day – 'keep calm and carry on' – while listening to Churchill's gravel voice growling defiance at the Nazis.

At least they took solace from the news that the *Graf Spee*, Germany's mighty battleship, had been scuppered in Montevideo harbour after being cornered by the Royal Navy. Then came the extraordinary morning when I watched a German fighter plane, a Messerschmidt 109, zooming over our house with smoke pouring from its engine. It flew so low that I could clearly see the pilot slumped in his cockpit, having failed to bail out. Moments later, an RAF Hurricane roared overhead, waggling its wings in a victory roll as the entire street came out to cheer.

Unlike my parents, it never occurred to me that we might lose the war. After all, we were British, weren't we? We just tightened our belts, learned to live with the sirens' banshee wail and looked forward to the days when we might once again feast on half-forgotten pre-war treats such as ice cream or bananas.

Meat, sugar, margarine, sweets, everything was rationed; yet I never felt deprived.

To feed his family my father dug up his lawn to grow King Edward potatoes and runner beans. There was also a henhouse full of Rhode Island Reds to relieve the diet of dried eggs that tasted like distemper, and a white rooster with the patriotic name of Winston, whom we ate for Christmas.

Although I was not a sickly infant, I still managed to contract every childhood disease going, from mumps and measles to whooping cough and chickenpox. At the age of seven, when the war had been going on for two years, I woke up one morning with a high temperature and a bright pink rash. Scarlet fever, said the doctor, and that evening I was wrapped in a blanket and taken by ambulance to an isolation ward in the Fever Hospital, a grim, prison-like building on Banstead Heath.

Denied all contact with my friends and family, I was held in quarantine for six long weeks, confined to bed for most of the time, and fed on a daily diet that never changed. As it was wartime, every morning began with a breakfast of cornflakes and powdered eggs. Lunch was boiled cod and potatoes – served without so much as a pinch of salt to render it vaguely palatable – followed by semolina pudding with no sugar, milk, or jam to help it down. No wonder that neither cod nor semolina have ever passed my lips since then.

Towards the end of my stay, I was finally allowed to play outside in the hospital grounds. It must have been in March because I remember catching two brimstone butterflies and preserving them like pressed flowers in one of my favourite books. At that moment in time, they were my most treasured belongings, but when at last I went home, my precious butterflies were taken away to be burned to prevent the spread of infection.

Eventually, after what seemed like a lifetime, I returned to the outside world and resumed my normal life. I learned how to whistle, play the jaws harp, and make catapults. The years passed and the seasons went around in a whirl of schoolboy crazes. Sometimes we amused ourselves by making what we called 'mud-bungers' out of pliable willow stems, to which we attached a lump of clay. When swung with a motion like that of an angler casting his bait, the mud-bunger released its missile which then hurtled through the air much further than we could ever have thrown it.

At junior school we played marbles and five-stones in the playground, swapped John Player cigarette cards and spent all our pocket money on sixpenny comics such as *The Beano* and *The Dandy*, whose characters included Korky the Cat and Desperate Dan, the world's strongest man, with his huge stubbly chin and fondness for Aunt Aggie's homemade cow pies.

When winter came and temperatures plummeted, we made slides, skidding down the frosty pavements until they shone like glass. When it snowed, we would go tobogganing after tea in the lamplit evenings, hurtling down roads whose surfaces had been packed down into icy pistes by passing traffic.

Christmas brought its own delights. In the run-up to the big day there were endless lengths of paper chains to be made, sticking each coloured link together until there were enough to decorate the dining room; and in the evenings a dozen of of us would go

carol singing around the houses, carrying candles in jam jars, and knocking on doors in the hope of receiving a sixpence or a hot mince pie.

Christmas Day itself always began with the ritual of delving into a stocking hung up the night before, to discover tangerines and brazil nuts, pink sugar mice with string tails, and chocolate money wrapped in gold paper. Only then would the serious business of unwrapping presents take place.

Lunch was always roast chicken served with bread sauce, sprouts and baked potatoes – the only day we ever ate such a luxurious dish – followed by Christmas pudding with a sprig of holly on top. Afterwards, when the curtains were drawn and the dining room had become a cave of warmth, we would sit by the fire, cracking walnuts and tucking into boxes of Batger's crystallised Chinese figs, a half-forgotten delicacy that only ever appeared at Christmastime.

In many ways Boxing Day was even better, when I would call on my best friend, Geoff Lanegan, and be invited in for a supper of cold turkey and mustard pickle washed down with glasses of Tizer, a soft drink with a distinctively zingy flavour sold under the slogan 'Tizer the Appetizer'.

I was only four years old when Geoff and I first met, not long after he and his family had arrived from Barking. He was a year older than me and, having been born within the sound of Bow Bells, was a true Londoner with an irrepressible cockney sense of humour.

His family were far better off than mine. In fact, they were the first people I knew who owned a car. Fred, his father, was a larger-than-life character in every way, an engineer in the printing trade, who had made several business trips to the States on board the *Queen Elizabeth*. In America he had acquired the habit of smoking fat cigars, which he waved around as he regaled us boys with tales of his exploits in New York and Chicago.

After one such transatlantic crossing he brought home a toy train set that was far superior to anything I had seen in England. Made by the Lionel Corporation in New York City, it had a string of blue coaches pulled by a magnificent steam locomotive that kept us amused for hours; but as soon as spring arrived the toys were packed away in the loft and we would head for Nonsuch to look for birds' nests.

Although egg collecting was not illegal in those days, we never took an egg until there were at least four in the nest – and woe betide anyone we caught in the act of removing an entire clutch. Using a blackthorn spine to pierce the egg at either end, we would place it gently to our lips and empty it by blowing out the yolk and albumen. Back home afterwards, each new find would be neatly labelled and placed with the rest of our collections in a shoebox on a bed of cotton wool.

We never discovered any rarities. They were all familiar garden species: blackbird, starling, robin, wood pigeon, but treasured, nonetheless. How I loved the song thrushes' nests, hidden deep in the hawthorn hedgerows, with their clay-lined cup and sky-blue eggs, and the more expert I became at finding them the greater became my knowledge of birds in general and their habitats. Without realising it, I was acquiring a passion for birdwatching and the natural world which has remained with me to this day.

But summer was the golden time. Released from school in mid-July, my pals and I could hardly wait to enter Nonsuch. Enclosed by galleon fleets of blowsy elms, its green acres were a schoolboy's paradise. Its unshorn meadows were our Wild West prairies, its hawthorn hedgerows our African bushveld.

Here, in the cow-parsley jungles whose hollow stems made brilliant pea-shooters, we built elaborate hideouts and became young Robin Hoods, stalking through the woods with our homemade bows and arrows, or swinging through the trees like demented gibbons, uttering the yodelling call made famous by Johnny Weissmuller, the Olympic swimmer and Hollywood actor who starred in a series of Tarzan films.

In one field, where a landmine had blown a deep crater in the clay, a pond had formed and nature, always swift to exploit a niche, moved in and colonised it with great crested newts – jam-jar dinosaurs with warty skins and sulphur bellies. Years later, I discovered that Dr David Bellamy, the conservationist who achieved lasting fame as the bounding botanist of BBC TV, used to catch newts in that same pond.

In late summer there were other treasures to be gleaned from the surrounding streets; apples and pears 'scrumped' from neighbours' gardens, and Victoria plums with purple skins and yellow flesh as sweet as sin.

All too soon the summer was over. In The Glade, the fallen leaves piled up by the kerbsides in knee-deep drifts, signalling the onset of autumn and the conker season. We soon learned where the best conkers could be gathered under the avenues in Nonsuch Park and, maintaining a sharp lookout for the park keepers, we would hurl sticks into the treetops where the chestnuts hung in ripening clusters until a lucky strike brought them raining down around our heads.

CHAPTER FOUR

NONSUCH was the perfect adventure playground, but it was not the real countryside. Somewhere beyond the surrounding sea of rooftops lay a wilder world where palm trees whispered in the breeze and basking sharks cruised beneath the cliffs in waters bluer than the Caribbean.

This I knew because one of the perks of my father's job with the Southern Railway was a limited number of privilege tickets which allowed him to take us on holiday to anywhere in Britain at no expense. So, while my childhood friends spent their summers at easy-to-reach south coast resorts such as Bognor or Littlehampton, we travelled by steam train down to Cornwall.

If somebody had told me I cut my first teeth on a Cornish pasty I would not have been surprised. All my childhood holidays were spent beyond the Tamar, and although I cannot have been more than three years old, I can still recall playing by a shallow stream running down to a beach near Mullion Cove. If I close my eyes, I can see it now. At the edge of the water, among spears of wild iris, a moorhen sits on her nest and everything is so vivid: the moorhen's scarlet sealing-wax beak, the yellow irises, the bubbling stream, the ever-beckoning Cornish sea.

Of course, this was long before the advent of package tours and cheap jet flights, in an age when the Mediterranean was still a rich man's playground. Yet, thanks to trains like the Cornish Riviera Express, you could reach Britain's own Côte d'Azur in just over six hours; and that is why, back in the long ago before the railways were nationalised, the biggest moment of my year was the day we set off for our family hols from Paddington.

The GWR – God's Wonderful Railway to its aficionados – was established in the 1830s, since when its main route to Penzance had become the most famous holiday line in the country and the Cornish Riviera Express, known to all GWR staff as 'The Limited', was its flagship service.

In the golden age of steam its elegant chocolate-and-cream carriages were hauled by King Class and Castle Class locomotives, painted a glossy Brunswick green and gleaming with polished brass, and since my father was a railwayman he would speak to the driver and I would be allowed on the footplate for a few precious moments as the fireman shovelled coal into the engine's blazing furnace.

Afterwards, standing in the corridor, nose glued to the window, I waited for the longed-for moment when the first glimpse of the sea appeared at Dawlish, framed to perfection by the red cliffs of south Devon. Then, as the train raced on to Plymouth and beyond, my mother would open our picnic lunch. Chicken sandwiches – such a treat in post-war Britain when the only other time we ever ate chicken was on Christmas Day!

On we went, huffing and puffing up Dainton Bank – the third steepest mainline incline in Britain – talking to the rails as we picked up speed with a hypnotic tiddly-tum rhythm on our way past the Dart at Totnes.

Crossing the Tamar on Brunel's mighty Royal Albert Bridge felt like travelling out of England into another country, a sense underlined when we reached St Ives, where even the street names had foreign-sounding names like Barnawoon and the locals addressed you as 'my 'andsome'.

Arriving at St Ives was the best bit of the whole day, having joined the branch line from St Erth as it wound its way around the coast, high above Carbis Bay and Porthminster beach until there it lay with its feet in the sea, the loveliest fishing port in the world.

This was the St Ives that had attracted generations of painters, drawn like moths to its pure Atlantic sea light in which everything – the painted boats, the pink hydrangeas, even the green and indigo waves – seemed twice as colourful. From Turner and Whistler to the present day, they have been bewitched by its matchless luminosity, dazzled by the reflective power of the encircling ocean.

In its heyday you might have seen 400 fishing boats in the harbour. But that was more than a century ago when the pilchard shoals still filled the bay like cloud shadows. 'Days of meat, money and light, all in one night,' the fishermen called them.

Even in the 1970s there was a living to be made and four men using hand lines could catch 400 stone of mackerel in a day. Yet long before then, in the St Ives I had come to know and love, the old-time net lofts and fish cellars had become artists' studios or were rented out to holiday visitors like ourselves.

Of course, none of this was known to me at the time. What held me in thrall was its uniquely higgledy-piggledy nature, a salt-encrusted barnacle of a town so totally different from my orderly suburban homeland, a Cornish *kasbah* of granite steps and crooked lanes with sudden glimpses of the sea.

Here I would make a beeline down to the lifeboat slipway where, next door to the 14th-century Sloop Inn, stood Hart's Dairy Ice

Cream Parlour and its splendid shop sign: '*Hart's Ice Cream. Often Licked. Never Beaten.*'

But most of the day would be spent on the white shell sands of Porthmeor, with my father in his one-piece black woollen bathing costume showing me how to catch the breakers on a plywood surfboard. No boogie boards in those days; no rashies or wetsuits to keep you warm. Instead, while my parents snoozed in hired deckchairs, I would lie on a towel and enjoy the delicious feeling of the sun drying the salty water on my back while herring gulls wailed above the town's lichen-scabbed rooftops.

One year, we forsook St Ives and spent a week on a farm in Rocky Valley, between Tintagel and Boscastle where the little River Trevillet tumbles down to the sea in a series of spectacular waterfalls. By day I went butterflying, catching silver-washed fritillaries as they basked on wild flowers at the water's edge; or dammed the river in the hope of catching the small brook trout that hovered in its shallow pools.

Another year we stayed at Polzeath on the Camel estuary. The taxi that took us from Wadebridge station drove straight onto the beach to show us the breakers rolling in before depositing us at the wooden chalet we had rented for the fortnight.

Nightingales sang on its roof every night, and the stream dribbling past through dense stands of cow parsley and yellow iris made its way down to the sands where, as I walked barefoot in its braided shallows, small dabs skittered away from under my toes.

In those days, even in the peak holiday season, the acres of sand between Pentire and the Greenaway were almost empty; just a few families scattered on each side of the bay, with beach towels and picnic baskets spread out on the rocks to mark their chosen territory.

The rocks themselves provided endless hours of exploration. Bristling with limpets and clusters of mussels, their shallow pools held all kinds of mysteries, from sea anemones with waving tentacles to shore crabs, blennies, and quick, darting prawns with translucent bodies. Elsewhere, beachcombing expeditions revealed hidden tidelines where small cowrie shells lay, and bigger pools deep enough to swim in.

On later visits to St Ives, as I grew older, I would leave my parents on Porthmeor beach, buy a pasty and a bottle of lemonade, and forsake the coast, following the foxglove lanes into the lonely moors of West Penwith, where the wind sang in the telephone wires above the patchwork fields and their Iron Age hedge banks set against the boundless ocean.

At Zennor, not far from the sphinx-shaped promontory of Gurnard's Head, a moorland brook ran under the road. Its clear waters were alive with trout, which I tried to catch by baiting a fish hook with a grasshopper and letting it slowly drift downstream, but always in vain.

Of course, we could never afford to stay for more than a fortnight. But one year, when the Blitz was at its height and our suburbs became a target for the Luftwaffe's nightly raids, I was evacuated to Cornwall.

CHAPTER FIVE

THE bomb had fallen in the night, close enough for the explosion to wake me as it shattered our windows and brought the lathe-and-plaster ceiling crashing down on my bed. Later, after the broken glass had been swept up, we sat down to breakfast in the kitchen and were just about to eat when a delayed-action bomb went off with such force that it blew the door off its hinges and sent it flying across the room.

That random air raid proved the catalyst for my evacuation, and a few days later I was despatched by train to Crockwood Farm, near Bude, with a gas mask around my neck, clutching a small suitcase with all my belongings and a few treasured books.

Even for those days, Crockwood was a small farm – no more than 35 acres of wheat, potatoes and wet meadows pitted by cows' hoof prints, where kingcups and cuckooflowers grew in spring and curlews stalked among the rushes, probing for worms with their long, curved bills. It belonged to Harold Brooks and his wife, and here I lived with their three children. Dark-haired Peggy was the oldest. Then came Cyril, who was roughly the same age as me, and Gordon, their youngest.

There was no bathroom, only a tin tub in front of the kitchen range, where us children were scrubbed on Friday nights, one by one, youngest first, to leap out afterwards onto the bare flagstone floor. Water was drawn, cold and pure, from a deep mossy well in the yard, and the lavatory was a limewashed shed at the bottom of the garden, where the *Daily Mirror* hung from a rusty nail in lieu of toilet paper and magpie moths with polka-dot wings shared the walls with spiders' webs.

No sirens disturbed the deep West Country hush. I fell asleep to the sound of owls in the woods and awoke to the triumphant clamour of the farmyard cockerel to begin a new life in an older, simpler world of oil lamps and flickering shadows, in which electricity had not yet arrived and the only source of power was Punch, the hammer-headed stallion who pulled the plough and transported us to Poughill church on Sundays, rumbling down the lanes in a painted cart.

For two years I never went to school. Instead, I fed the pigs their daily slops, lifted potatoes until my back felt broken, hunted for hens' eggs in the nettle beds, and learned to milk the cows, leaning my forehead against their warm flanks while swallows twittered in the rafters and the pail foamed white between my knees.

My worst chore was mucking out Punch's stable. In harness he was a willing and docile worker, but in his stable he became an equine Jekyll and Hyde who would roll back his bloodshot eyes and then lash out with his huge hind legs.

Like the rest of the family, I was fed on hearty meals of rabbit pie and chipple pasties (made with onions instead of the traditional beef, potato and swede), but I was always hungry. Perhaps it was because of the meagre breakfasts – Kellogg's Puffed Wheat or crusts soaked in milk. Throughout my long sojourn, despite gathering a pail-full of new-laid eggs every day, only once was I given one for my breakfast. The rest all went to market. So outdoors I would go, stealing carrots from the garden, walking barefoot through the orchard grass to fill my pockets with windfall apples and feast on hedgerow blackberries until my face and hands were purple.

Only once did I ever see the sea, although it was less than two miles away. That was when an American cargo ship loaded with PX stores for the troops went aground and broke up on the rocks. Like old-time wreckers, people from far and wide hurried down to the beach intent on plunder. Scattered along the tideline I found tins of peanuts, canned pineapples (an undreamed-of luxury in wartime Britain), and boxes of Wrigley's spearmint chewing gum.

I ended the day being violently sick, but a neighbouring farmer fared even worse. Having waded into the surf to haul a heavy wooden packing case ashore, he managed to manhandle it onto his wagon and made off as fast as his horse could trot. Once safely home, he broken open the case with a crowbar, hoping to find a small fortune in cigarettes – only to discover it was full of wet toilet rolls.

On the days when Peggy and Cyril went off to school, I would go exploring around the farm. For a little boy from suburban Surrey, the surrounding fields were full of wonders: wrens' nests, adders, orange-tip butterflies with glowing wings and purple orchids with spotted leaves.

Dividing the fields were massive hedge banks of Cornish slate, each one a linear jungle of ferns and foxgloves, shaded by wind-bent thorns and riddled with rabbit burrows. The rabbits were a nuisance. They laid waste the young corn like locusts, but they were also a valuable wartime source of protein. Every evening I would help set the gin traps, pressing down the rusty spring to open their jaws and expose the plate on which a rabbit might unwittingly tread; and early next morning I would rush out through the dew-soaked grass to collect the night's catch, despatch the victims with a blow at the back of the head as I had been taught, and remove their entrails with a jackknife.

Even more exciting was rabbiting at harvest time. As the old-fashioned reaper-binder clattered around the cornfields, the rabbits retreated into the ever-diminishing island of standing corn left in the middle, until one by one they would break from cover and run across the stubble, pursued by gangs of boys with dogs and sticks.

None of this struck me as even remotely barbaric at the time. Small boys are themselves like predatory animals with the hunting instinct burning in their veins, and I accepted without question the unsentimental ways of the countryside. But then an incident occurred that would change my views for ever.

It happened one spring morning, when a badger dig took place in the bluebell wood beyond the orchard. A dozen men had gathered at the farm with dogs, shovels, crowbars, and stoneware crocks of cider for the day's sport. Off to the wood we trooped until we came to a mossy bank where the badgers had made their sett, tunnelling deep into the loam. A terrier was put down one of the holes and silence settled on the wood. Then from below ground came the sound of furious fighting.

Moments later the terrier emerged, torn and bleeding, followed by the black and white mask of an angry badger. At once one of the men leapt forward and grabbed it by the neck with a pair of tongs, while another clubbed it with a pick handle. The badger coughed, twitched, and then hung limp as the cider was passed around and somewhere deeper in the wood a blackbird sang a requiem as we retraced our steps and turned for home. The senseless cruelty I had witnessed continued to haunt me for a long time afterwards, and I sometimes wonder if that brutal act was the trigger that first set me on the road to becoming a conservationist.

Most days, though, the farm had few visitors. The only exception was Sid the quarryman, who regularly turned up for a lunch of pasty or rabbit pie. I loved to watch him light his cigarette by placing the end over the oil lamp's glass cover, after which he would sit back with a deep sigh and blow smoke rings at the ceiling.

I think he must have taken a shine to me. 'Where's that little tacker of your'n?' he would enquire of Mrs Brooks in his rich Cornish accent, and once made me a flute, whittled from a green ash branch, which became one of my most precious possessions.

The months rolled by and I missed my parents with an unbearable longing made worse by the distant sound of steam trains in the valley, knowing they were heading upcountry to within a few miles of my home.

Every now and then a parcel would arrive from Stoneleigh, sometimes prompted by not-so-subtle reminders, as this extract from a letter written at the time reveals:

Dear Mummy,

Thank you for the comic and could you send some chocolate. Daisy, one of the cows has got a calf it is a bull. The pig will have a litter soon. Cyril nearly got bitten by an adder when he was tilling his rabbit traps. One day I helped Mr Brooks drive the sheep down to Poughill. I hope I get some nice birthday presents. With love from Brian xxx

Winter passed. The magpies' nests were roofed with thorns and spring soon turned into summer, yet there seemed no end in sight to my exile. The year crawled on and I might have stayed even longer had it not been for the day I fell out of the farm cart and broke my right arm just above the wrist. Hurriedly, I was taken off to the cottage hospital at Stratton, but they could do nothing there. 'He'll have to go up to Exeter,' said the doctor, and so I did.

On arriving in Exeter Hospital, the first thing that happened was that I was stood in a bath and given an enema. I can only imagine that, faced with the sight of this grubby urchin with his unkempt hair and flea-bitten legs, they decided to clean me up, inside and out, before putting my broken arm in plaster and popping me into one of their spotless white hospital beds.

There, I was finally reunited with my parents, who I had not seen for nearly two years, and taken back to Briarwood Road and the Blitz with an accent so broadly Cornish that even my mother could barely understand me. But once I was home it soon fell away and I returned to school none the worse for my adventures, apart from a complete inability to understand mathematics that I have never been able to cure.

At the time I was overjoyed to be home and reunited with Geoff and Vic and the rest of my long-lost pals. Only now do I realise how lucky I was. I did not know it then, but for two long years I had belonged to a way of life which has long since followed the heavy horse into oblivion. Hardship there was, and cruelty, too, as I witnessed in the wood where the badger died. But there was also beauty and dignity in full measure, and the awakening of a love of all things wild which has stayed with me to this day. It was, I suppose, an unhappy time for an eight-year-old, all alone and far from home, but its magic haunts me still.

CHAPTER SIX

BY the time I returned home the war was drawing to its close. Another summer was beginning, and my suburban surroundings had never seemed lovelier or more welcoming. The only major change was the presence of Keith, my new baby brother, who had been born in 1942 while I was still in Cornwall.

Two years later, to everybody's surprise – even my parents, I suspect – my youngest brother Nigel came into the world. Because of the age gap between us, I regarded them both as pests and had as little as possible to do with them. (Only in later life, when the age difference had disappeared, did we become the best of friends.)

Otherwise, life went on much as it had done before, except that potato peelings and leftover scraps were placed in the bins that now stood by the roadsides and were emptied each week to be used as pig food. The sirens continued to fill the air with their banshee wail, and I slept every night in our air-raid shelter.

Two kinds of domestic shelters were available during the war. One was the Anderson shelter, a cheap and cheerful construction named after Sir John Anderson, who was in control of Air Raid Precautions (ARP). Made of curved metal sheets bolted together, they were half-buried in the back garden with earth piled high on top. They were dark and damp and smelt of wet concrete, but I always wished we had one despite their tendency to flood.

The alternative was the Morrison shelter, the one we had chosen, introduced in 1941 by Herbert Morrison, the Home

Secretary. This was a heavy steel table with detachable wire mesh sides and offered a much more comfortable night's sleep because it was built indoors.

When the sirens sounded, I would crawl inside, taking with me my most prized possession – a stuffed armadillo mounted on a wooden board. I had bought it in a St Ives antique shop for what seemed to me the enormous price of five shillings. The shop owner told me how it had aroused the curiosity of American soldiers based nearby. 'They were always boasting about how everything in America was bigger and better,' he said. 'So, when they asked me what it was, I told them it was just a St Ives flea.'

By now the Nazis had unleashed a terrifying new weapon of indiscriminate mass destruction against Britain in the forlorn hope that it might break our spirit and turn the tide of war. First launched in June 1944, this was the 'doodlebug', a flying bomb powered by a jet engine that announced its arrival with an unmistakable growling sound. When the engine stopped, you knew the flying bomb was about to fall from the sky and explode a few seconds later.

Even when the war was at its height it was quite normal for children to play in the streets. One afternoon, on my way back from Nonsuch Park with my pals, we heard the drone of an incoming doodlebug just as we were crossing the London Road. Its sinister silhouette was clearly visible, and it seemed to be heading straight towards us.

Without thinking we ran for cover, diving headlong over someone's front garden wall to lie flat on the ground behind it. Moments later we heard the engine cut out and waited for the inevitable explosion with our hands over our ears. Luckily for us it fell short of the road and blew up in the field on the other side, after which we got up, dusted down our grubby knees and went home for tea. Just another day in wartime suburbia.

In my absence and despite the menace of the doodlebugs, time had healed the scars of war. Neglected shrubs and garden flowers ran riot amid the rubble, transforming bomb sites into a wasteland of raspberry canes, golden rod, and dense jungles of rosebay willowherb in which, sometimes, like the ruins of a lost city, we would stumble across a garden statue or a marble sundial half-choked in weeds. And over it all, like a cheap perfume, hung the cloying scent of mauve-flowering buddleia bushes.

This was the summer of the great invasion, not by Rommel's panzers but by swarms of butterflies. In Nonsuch Park, trenches had been dug across the open fields to prevent German planes landing. In doing so they exposed the brick drains of King Henry's forgotten palace, together with shards of stoneware pots; but the real treasures were the butterflies. Attracted by the massed ranks of flowering thistles that sprang unbidden from the clay, small tortoiseshells arrived in numbers beyond counting; and as the summer advanced, peacocks, commas, painted ladies, red admirals and clouded yellows poured across the Channel to join them, settling on every back-garden buddleia where they clung in clusters, drinking the nectar with watch-spring tongues until they were too drunk to fly.

Today they are just a memory: bomb sites, air-raid shelters, butterflies, and all. In Dorset, where I live now, my garden buddleias still attract the red admirals. But whenever I return to my suburban roots, now fully restored and more prosperous than ever with their carports and loft conversions, my mind runs back to those butterfly years when the sun shone all day long and the buddleias bloomed, and summers seemed as if they could never end.

CHAPTER SEVEN

ON 8th May 1945, about a week after Adolf Hitler had committed suicide in his Berlin bunker, Germany unconditionally surrendered. Church bells rang out across the country and all Europe celebrated VE day.

Who could forget the day the word went around that there were bananas in the shops again, or the long queues that formed as we waited for the long-lost taste of a Lyons ice cream cornet? Yet although the war was over austerity continued, and it would be another nine years before food rationing ended.

In Briarwood I never felt that we were poor, but we still lived without a car, fridge, washing machine or telephone. Nor did we have a TV set. Instead, I spent most evenings with my ears glued to the wireless, waiting for the catchy theme tune called 'Devil's Galop' which introduced every episode of *Dick Barton – Special Agent* and was followed in 1953 by *Journey into Space*, the BBC's first-ever sci-fi series.

The first TV programme I ever saw was at my friend Vic Carr's house in The Glade. There, on a flickering, black-and-white, nine-inch screen, I watched Derby County beat Charlton Athletic in extra time to win the 1946 FA Cup Final. As for us at 34 Briarwood Road, we had to wait until the 1950s before the old Bakelite wireless with its Art Deco sunburst facia was replaced on its shelf in the dining room corner by our first TV set.

Meanwhile, comics such as *The Hotspur* and *The Wizard* had been overtaken in popularity by *Eagle*, which was also influenced by the growing interest in science fiction. Published in 1950 by the Hulton Press, it was founded by Marcus Morris, a Lancastrian vicar, and featured the galactic adventures of Dan Dare, its lean-jawed hero, and his nemesis, the Mekon, a wicked alien with an enormous green dome of a forehead.

By now I had graduated to Junior School, which still involved a mile walk there and back every day. The headmaster, Mr Burston, and Miss Harding, my class teacher, both encouraged my growing passion for natural history to the point where I was once invited to lead a school expedition into Nonsuch Park to point out a green woodpecker's nest I had found in a hollow tree.

A school report at the time ended with the following remarks: *'Brian has an unusually good memory and a very marked ability for drawing. He shows great interest, especially in nature and takes a valuable part in all oral lessons but needs to work especially hard in arithmetic.'*

Because the playing fields had been dug up to prevent German gliders landing there, our sporting activities were confined to games of rounders in the playground. At playtime, while the girls swung their skipping ropes, we boys used to hang upside down by our feet from the school railings or play 'King-he', an improvised version of tag involving a tennis ball, in which one player was chosen to be 'It'. His task was to throw the ball at the other players. Anyone he hit had to join him until only one was left to be declared the winner. What made the game even more fun was the rule whereby you could avoid being hit by punching the ball away – usually with a handkerchief wrapped around your fist to prevent sore knuckles.

Those playground games were tremendous fun. So was roller skating up and down Briarwood when cars were still an uncommon sight and we could zoom happily down the middle of the road, hands clasped nonchalantly behind our backs; but the highlight of the week in post-war Stoneleigh was the regular Saturday morning picture show at the Rembrandt Cinema. Put on specially for children, these mid-morning matinees became hugely popular, and no wonder. For an admission price of sixpence, you could look forward to at least a couple of hours of cartoons and adventure films.

My all-time favourite cartoons were those created by Looney Tunes, featuring Tweety and Sylvester the Cat, who always seemed to come off worst. They were followed by comedies such as *The Three Stooges* (Curly, Larry and Moe), and most popular of all, westerns starring Roy Rogers and Gene Autry.

How we cheered our heroes; how we booed the baddies! Sometimes the noise was so great you could hardly hear the soundtrack; but mostly the audience was well behaved. Inevitably, though, there were exceptions, leading to the day we were all frisked before being allowed into the main body of the cinema. The result was a sofa in the foyer piled high with confiscated pea-shooters, catapults, and cap pistols.

Not that I ever owned a cap gun. In wartime most of us whittled six-shooters out of bits of wood, or simply pointed our fingers at each other. As for my dream of owning the 'Red Indian' war bonnet of imitation eagle feathers displayed in the window of a Ewell Court toyshop, the price remained far beyond anything my parents could afford. The best I could muster was an Apache-style bandana with a solitary chicken feather stuck in it.

In summer we still went to Cornwall for our holidays, although there were now five of us, and a photograph taken at the time by my mother shows us on Polzeath beach, with my father at one end with me and Keith in the middle, and Nigel, a grizzling toddler, at the other end.

At home, meanwhile, my passion for natural history continued to grow apace. With Geoff Lanegan, my inseparable companion, we unearthed stag beetles in the rotting hulks of fallen elms and discovered the secret corners of Nonsuch Park where green hairstreaks and other butterflies could be caught, and spent hours pinning our trophies on setting boards until their wings hardened and they were ready to join the peacocks and red admirals in our collection boxes.

I will never forget the joy of seeing my first clouded yellow – a summer migrant from across the Channel – or the day I nearly caught a monarch. With a wingspan of up to four inches, this handsome insect is our largest butterfly and one of our rarest, so imagine my excitement when I saw one settled beneath the chestnut avenue in Nonsuch Park.

There it rested in all its glory, its bright orange wings with their bold black veins and polka-dot borders, a perfect match for the illustration in my copy of *Butterflies of the British Isles*. I had no net with me, only my school cap which I held in both hands as I approached, step by cautious step, hardly daring to breathe.

For one triumphant moment I had it trapped; but somehow it managed to escape and fly up to the crown of a chestnut tree, leaving me to stare through tears of frustration at the dusting of scales its wings had left on the inside of my cap.

Although moths never had quite the same glamour, we had both begun to collect their larvae, feeding them in jam jars until they pupated. One of our best hunting grounds was Briarwood Road itself, where privet hawk moth caterpillars gave away their presence by leaving their droppings clearly visible on the pavements. All we had to do was to find their favourite food plants – either privet or lilac – then look up into the overhanging foliage to find them, fat green monsters the size of my fingers, clinging tightly to the underside of the leaves.

But it was birds that always held the greatest appeal. When butterflying was over, I loved to walk in Nonsuch Park just to hear the creaking voices of grey partridges calling in the autumn dusk. One year I spotted a great grey shrike, a rare winter vagrant. As I followed it down the frost-laden hedgerows I tasted the same joy I had experienced when seeing the monarch and stalked it for miles, never wanting to let it out of my sight.

It must have been about that same time that I saw my first kingfisher near Ewell Springs, the source of the Hogsmill River that flows north through Malden to meet the Thames at Kingston. Bubbling up from the underlying chalk, the springs created a series of ponds in whose crystal waters I used to catch sticklebacks and carry them home in a jam jar.

Having flowed under the Chessington Road from the old village horse pond, the waters provided the power for a flour mill whose brick and timber façade overlooked the river's uppermost reaches, and it was here that I spotted this living jewel perched on an overhanging hazel bough.

With its rufous breast and iridescent blue feathers, it was like an alien from some faraway tropical world. Until then I had no idea that kingfishers lived within a mile of my home. I could not wait to tell Geoff of my discovery, and from then on, the Hogsmill's limpid headwaters became one of our regular birdwatching haunts.

CHAPTER EIGHT

IN 1946 I sensed I was beginning to grow up. I was now nearly 12 years old. Before I knew it, I would be a teenager and the idea did not appeal to me. At least I had long since swapped my trike for a proper bicycle, a grown-up's two-wheeler with a crossbar. Mine was a Hercules, which I soon learned to ride without holding the handlebars, arms raised above my head as if taming a bucking bronco. How I envied friends of mine who owned more expensive models such as those made by Claud Butler, with their derailleur gears, drop handlebars and lightweight frames made of Reynolds 531 alloy steel tubing; but my trusty old workhorse served me well.

That same year with some trepidation I had sat my 11-plus exams, knowing how my understanding of maths was almost beyond salvation after two missed years of schooling in Cornwall; but somehow, thanks largely to long evenings of extra coaching I managed to scrape through.

The reward was acceptance at Rutlish Grammar School in Merton Park. I had wanted to go to Glyn Grammar, a progressive new school only a short bus ride away in Epsom, but my parents insisted that I would receive a better education at Rutlish, a much older establishment that saw itself as a kind of minor public school, complete with prefects and a house system, where the masters wore gowns and mortar boards. Among its alumni were John Major, who became the leader of the Conservative Party and Prime Minister from 1990 to 1997, Tubby Hayes, Britain's greatest jazz saxophonist, and Neville Heath, a notorious serial killer hung for murder in 1946.

Getting there involved taking the train from Stoneleigh to Wimbledon and catching the branch line service to Merton Park. Furthermore, I argued, I would be a total stranger as all my chums were going to Epsom. Worst of all, Rutlish was a rugger school.

This was a particularly hard blow as I had just become a mad keen soccer fan. Until then I think my father was disappointed that I appeared to show no interest in ball games. Imagine his surprise, therefore, when I agreed to go with Geoff to watch West Ham play Chelsea at Stamford Bridge. Having been a lifelong West Ham supporter, Fred Lanegan had obtained tickets, and so off we went on a typically dull winter day.

In no time we were part of the biggest crowd I had ever seen, and from where we stood, looking across the stadium to the terraces on the other side, I could see the massed ranks of supporters lighting up Woodbines that shone like glow-worms in the gathering gloom.

Moments later the waiting was over as Chelsea ran out to a deafening round of applause, followed by West Ham in their traditional claret and blue strip. I knew little about football but even I had heard of Tommy Lawton, Chelsea's international centre forward. Now, there he was, limbering up on the pitch far below, hair parted down the middle and a number nine emblazoned on his blue shirt.

As I watched, the ball came to him and he thumped it solidly from about 20 yards out, striking the crossbar with such force that it continued to shake for several seconds as the crowd roared their approval and, in that single moment before the game had even kicked off, I knew I was hooked for life. The fact that the match ended in a 2–2 draw was irrelevant. I was going to be a professional footballer like Tommy Lawton, score stupendous goals and soak up the acclaim of 60,000 delirious fans.

Back home again I borrowed my father's size-seven boots with their heavy leather toecaps and hurried off to the park with Geoff and the rest of our gang to play seven-a-side kickabouts with our coats piled up for goal posts.

But how could I realise my new-found dream when rugby was the game at Rutlish? I begged my father to change his mind. Surely, having played top-class amateur football for Wimbledon, he must understand? It was no use; and in September when the autumn term started, I set off for Merton in my new school uniform, my legs imprisoned for the first time in long grey flannel trousers.

I hated Rutlish from the moment I saw it, and further acquaintance did nothing to change my mind. Within its gaunt Victorian red-brick carcass was an assembly hall that doubled as a gym, complete with wall bars, where we gathered for morning prayers led by the headmaster, Mr Blenkinsop, followed by a rendition of the school song with its dreary chorus:

> *Up, boys! Truest fame*
> *Lies in high endeavour.*
> *Play the game! Keep the flame*
> *Burning brightly ever!*
> *Up, boys, play the game! Up! – and on!*

(Not until later did I learn the alternative playground version that began with the words: '*Balls to Mr Blenkinsop.*')

Elsewhere in the main building, flights of stone stairs led to a science laboratory where sixth-form students dissected frogs, a series of classrooms filled with heavy, wooden desks on which past generations of pupils had carved their initials, and the art room on the top floor.

A short distance away lay the sports field where I was given my first introduction to rugby football. The teacher in charge was also my maths master. He had recognised what a duffer I was at numeracy and now he was going to teach this stupid blond kid a lesson.

'You,' he said, pointing to the biggest boy in the class and handing him the ball, 'are going to run as fast as you can to the end of the pitch.' Then he turned to me. 'And you are going to stop him.'

The intention was quite clear. He was determined to show me up in front of the whole class. What he did not know was that I was used to throwing myself about, something I had learned when playing goalie during our football kickabouts.

The boy with the ball was a hefty lad almost twice my size, but it made no difference. As he tried to swerve past me, I launched myself through the air and clamped my arms around his knees. He went down as if poleaxed, with me on top of him while my classmates cheered, and the maths master looked on in disbelief.

That episode earned me respect but never really endeared me to rugby. There were aspects of the game I quite enjoyed but I had already given my soul to football, the game so despised by my teachers for its working-class roots.

Somehow, despite my total inability to understand mathematics or the mysteries of algebra, I managed to survive my first two years. I buckled down to the long hours of homework and even got used to the daily commute from Stoneleigh. At least it gave me the opportunity to watch the express trains racing through Wimbledon station on their way down to Bournemouth and the West Country.

Hauled by the powerful steam locomotives of that era, they were a magnificent sight: King Arthur, Lord Nelson, and the streamlined Merchant Navy class engines clad in the straight-sided casing that earned them the derogatory nickname of Spam Cans.

Meanwhile, life carried on as best it could in the aftermath of the war. At weekends I still hung out with Geoff and the rest of my Stoneleigh friends, swimming at the public baths in Epsom and treating ourselves to twopenny bags of crackling at the fish and chip shop on the way home.

To pay for such luxuries I had taken on a Sunday morning paper round at Atkinson's corner shop on the Broadway which earned me the princely sum of half a crown a week – more than enough for an evening at the pictures and a packet of Butterkist popcorn, or a sweet-shop treat such as a sherbet fountain with a liquorice straw.

So far, sex had not yet reared its head. Girls were mysterious creatures, an alien species who belonged in a parallel universe quite separate from ours, and although we were vaguely aware of the act itself, we were still totally ignorant of the basic mechanics.

Although not yet teenagers, we thought nothing of travelling up to London by ourselves to spend a day at Regent's Park Zoo or the Natural History Museum in South Kensington. After one such excursion we emerged from Morden tube station at the end of the day to find that a dense fog had come down since we left, and all bus services had been cancelled, leaving us no option but to stumble back home through the murk to Stoneleigh, a good four miles away.

Similar events happened every winter, when spells of cold weather combined with windless conditions, allowing dense clouds of airborne pollutants to build up over Greater London. Most of it arose from the use of cheap lignite coal in the early post-war years, not to mention the presence of several giant coal-fired power stations such as the one at Battersea. In addition, further pollutants were pumped out by vehicle exhausts, steam locomotives and the diesel-fuelled buses which had replaced the old network of electric trams and trolleybuses.

The result became known as smog, an acrid yellow gloom that was so thick you could barely see your hand in front of your face, and whose sulphurous reek caught the back of the throat. Such 'pea-soupers' were nothing new. I had known them all my life, but they were getting worse, and in 1952 they would culminate in the Great Smog of London, the worst air-pollution event in our history, resulting in 12,000 deaths and, four years later, Britain's first Clean Air Act.

Fortunately, no such calamities spoiled the summer of 1948 when Britain hosted the Olympic Games, and it could not have come at a better time to boost the nation's morale. London was still scarred by acres of bomb sites that not even the natural invasion of flowering buddleia jungles could hide. Bread rationing continued right up until a month before the Games began. Britain itself was flat broke and the competing athletes even had to bring their own towels with them. No wonder the 1948 Summer Olympics became known as the Austerity Games.

This was the year that saw the nationalisation of Britain's railways, the opening of the country's first supermarket and the birth of the National Health Service.

Dinah Shore was singing 'Buttons and Bows', Pee Wee Hunt and his orchestra topped the charts with their rendition of 'Twelfth Street Rag', and Manchester United beat Blackpool 4–2 in the FA Cup Final.

The Games themselves were opened by King George VI and I was there to watch two days of athletics events at Wembley Stadium. Somehow my Uncle Fred had managed to buy tickets for my cousin and me for the princely sum of 3s 6d each, and what I remember most vividly is the thrill of being part of the crowd overlooking the sacred turf beneath Wembley's famous twin towers and watching Emil Zátopek, Czechoslovakia's great middle-distance runner, make his Olympic debut.

The 'Bouncing Czech', as the press called him, became one of the greatest athletes of all time and went on to take the 5,000 and 10,000 metres gold medals at the 1952 Games in Helsinki. But the biggest star was the Dutch sprinter, Fanny Blankers-Koen. Dressed in her running vest and bright orange knickers, this 30-year-old mother of two won four gold medals and became known, inevitably, as 'The Flying Housewife'.

CHAPTER NINE

FOR three more years after the Olympics, I continued my grammar school education at Rutlish. Sometimes, when school life became overwhelming, I used to escape from it by immersing myself in *Tarka the Otter* by Henry Williamson, whose lyrical descriptions of my beloved West Country became a form of release from the stuffy confines of my classroom. Dipping into its pages I soon found myself transported to the Atlantic cliffs of Baggy Point among the seals and ravens, or watching buzzards sailing over the Torridge oak woods; and unknowingly, perhaps for the first time in my life, I felt myself moved by the sheer power of words.

Yet much as I adored the Southwest, I found my allegiance sorely tested when my uncle George Vestey and his family moved to Derbyshire, having found a job with a chemical company in Darley Dale, near Matlock.

With my cousin Peter I spent many a happy school holiday there, running wild in the countryside with our bows and arrows like fugitives from Sherwood Forest. In retrospect I sometimes wonder why we were not reprimanded by the police, as our homemade arrows were potentially lethal, being tipped with the brass casings of .303 rifle bullets after their lead core had been stripped out.

It wasn't long before we had made friends with Norman Stone, a local lad with a broad north country accent who showed us how to tickle trout in a clear stream that came bubbling out of the clough, a deep cleft in the hillsides. In return we showed him how to balance like circus artists on empty tar barrels and roll them along the flat tops of the evil-smelling chemical waste tips near the factory where our uncle worked.

This was my first glimpse of the north country, and as we drove around with my uncle in his posh Jaguar sports car, I marvelled at the muscular beauty of its limestone dales. In Matlock I gazed in awe at the soaring cliff face of High Tor, watched shoals of grayling ghosting under the stone bridge at Bakewell and came home in time to hear the curlews calling as the sun sank behind the gritstone edges of Stanton Moor.

By now I had become a Rutlish rebel, refusing to join their Junior Cadet Force or play rugby on Saturdays for the school's second fifteen because I had now joined Stoneleigh Wanderers' football team. Realising I would never become a mathematician, the school staff had given up and allowed me to spend more time in the art room, pursuing the one subject at which I excelled above all others. As a result, I won the Louisa Bennet Prize, an annual award for the school's most gifted artist.

I also loved English, a subject in which I was encouraged by our form master, Frank Tole. Once, having been given the usual essay subject, '*What I did on my holidays*', I described the thrill of our annual train journey down to Cornwall, in which I can recall using a phrase about 'herons hunched at the tide's edge' to describe the scene as we skirted the Exe estuary on the way down to Dawlish. 'Boys,' cried Frank Tole to my great embarrassment, 'we have a writer among us!'

As for other subjects, I enjoyed history and geography but found learning French almost impossible with its strangulated vowels and rolling 'rrrrr' sounds – until my Uncle Fred announced that he was taking me and my cousin Peter to Paris for a week.

This was my first time abroad and I could not have been in better hands. Uncle Fred had that rare knack of being able to communicate with us at our level without ever losing his firm sense of parental authority. He was mad on jazz and cricket and spoke with a Michael Caine accent overlaid with a gravel timbre due to his constant smoking – an addiction that would eventually kill him – and even though he was a Londoner born and bred, he had been to Paris before and loved the city almost as much as his own.

Being so soon after the war, I was conscious that we were on a tight budget. We stayed at a small rented apartment off the Boulevard Saint Michel, where I was given my first lesson in the wonders of French cuisine. 'They don't do eggs and bacon here,' Fred had warned us as we sat down to breakfast. 'I'm afraid it's just bread and coffee.'

I remember thinking how unappetising that would be. Until our *petit dejeuner* arrived, a wicker basket with crusty baguettes, home-made apricot jam, and a yellow slab of Normandy butter. If that was a revelation, the *café au lait* served in eight-sided cups was even more so – especially as I had only ever known the taste of Camp Coffee at home!

My exploration of French cuisine continued at lunchtime when I looked at the menu and chose a *salade de tomates*. Imagine my consternation when it arrived, consisting of nothing but a plate of sliced tomatoes! This was nothing like the salads I was served up at home. Where was the lettuce, the hard-boiled egg, the spring onions and sliced beetroot topped with a dollop of Heinz Salad Cream?

Then I took a mouthful and my taste buds exploded as, for the first time in my life, I was introduced to a classic French dressing with its mingled flavours of garlic and olive oil, together with those of wine vinegar, parsley and chopped shallot.

With Fred as our guide, we explored all the city's wondrous sights, from Napoleon's solid porphyry tomb in Les Invalides to the Eiffel Tower and the pigeon's-eye views from the Sacre Coeur at the top of Montmartre. Embalmed in the city's unique smell, half garlic and half Gauloises cigarette smoke, we travelled everywhere on the Métro, emerging to stroll along the banks of the Seine or seek out the crags and waterfalls of the Parc des Buttes Chaumont, the fifth-largest green space in Paris but also the least known to visitors.

By the end of the week, I had absorbed enough of France to add a pass in French to my seven O levels. More than that, it had aroused my curiosity about the wider world, and an overwhelming determination to see more of it that would eventually change the whole direction of my life.

Having excelled at painting and drawing, I had always imagined that, when I left school, I would go to art college, but my father had other ideas. 'You'll end up painting nudes in a St Ives backstreet,' he said scornfully. 'What kind of career is that?'

I thought it sounded rather good, but he was not to be moved, and so at the age of 16 I left Rutlish without a clue as to what my future might hold. I knew only that without maths or Latin there was little point in continuing my education. Nor did Rutlish have a careers master in those days, and that is how I started work as a messenger boy in London.

My employers were Leonard Hill, the publishers of a raft of technical magazines including the wonderfully descriptive *Muck Shifter and Public Works Digest*.

Leonard Hill himself was a self-made man, a pint-sized martinet who ruled the office with a rod of iron and once issued an order to all his staff forbidding them to use more than two sheets of toilet paper at a time. He had excelled at selling advertising space, which was how his company made money, and my job as a messenger was the first rung of a five-year training scheme. Its stated objective was to produce an endless stream of space salesmen and would-be editors, but it was really little more than an ingenious scheme to obtain cheap labour for the more mundane office jobs.

With my fellow trainees I turned up every morning at head office in Oxford Street, passing the paper seller on the pavement outside, whose mournful voice never changed whatever the headlines: 'News-Star-Standard,' he announced dolefully to the world at large, 'Annuver murder!'

When lunchtime came, we would make our way to the nearest greasy-spoon café, usually run by cheerful Italians with a kitchen downstairs from which food would arrive on a dumb waiter; or else we saved up our luncheon vouchers and splurged them all on chicken curry at a Chinese restaurant – another new experience for me.

My job, for which I was paid the princely sum of three pounds and ten shillings a week, involved daily bus trips from the head office in Oxford Street to the accounts department in Hampstead.

On one such journey I was sitting upstairs on the bus as it made its way down Fleet Street. The rest of the upper deck was empty, and so I felt nothing but mildly surprised when a middle-aged man in a fawn raincoat sat down beside me. I moved my briefcase onto my lap to make more space and then to my annoyance felt his thigh pushing up against mine as if needing still more room. Only then did I notice he had exposed himself.

For a moment I froze as mixed feelings of shock and revulsion surged through me. Then, without thinking, I raised my briefcase and brought it crashing down on his groin. As he screamed in agony, I shoved past him and jumped off the bus while it was still crawling down Fleet Street. The last I saw of him was his doubled-up silhouette in the upstairs back window.

At home, meanwhile, football had taken over my life and I could not wait for the season to begin. Unlike the old kickabouts in Nonsuch Park, where we used to pile up our coats as makeshift goal posts, I had spent three years playing in the local junior league on proper pitches with goal nets, corner flags and even an accredited referee, until I was 17, when my father arranged a trial for me with Wimbledon Juniors at their old home ground in Plough Lane. Throughout that season, wearing the shirt with the centre forward's number nine on my back, I began to realise my potential. Thanks to the coaching of Alec Fuce, the former first-team player who was now our manager, I began scoring goals on a regular basis and ended the season with what I felt was my best performance, scoring a hat-trick in a 7–2 victory over Dulwich Hamlet Juniors.

The next season might have seen me progressing to the reserves or even as far as the first 11; but in April 1953 my footballing career was put on hold. National Service was looming, and after celebrating my last night of freedom by snogging with the office belle in St James's Park, I joined the Royal Navy.

CHAPTER TEN

WHEN the Second World War ended in 1945, Britain faced the problem of what to do with the millions of servicemen who had been called up to defend their country. Naturally enough, they were fed up with war. They had been told they were fighting for freedom, and now they wanted it for themselves. To a man, they yearned for 'Civvy Street' and just wanted to go home. But who would fill the gaps in the ranks when the wartime conscripts were demobbed?

Prime Minister Clement Atlee was the man who grasped the nettle of peacetime conscription. His Labour government, elected largely on the strength of the 'khaki' vote, was now honour bound to bring the men home. Then, faced with the twin evils of a deteriorating international situation and the possibility of unrest in the ranks, Atlee was forced to introduce a National Service Bill in March 1947, making every male citizen between the ages of 18 and 26 liable for compulsory military service.

When the Bill was passed, conscription was for only 12 months, but within a year it had been extended to 18 months and in 1950 the war in Korea produced a further amendment, increasing national service to two years. Although introduced in 1947, national service was overwhelmingly a phenomenon of the 1950s. It belonged to the Age of Austerity, along with prefabs, Standard Vanguard cars, Brylcreem, drape-suited Teddy boys, *The Goon Show* on the BBC and Kay Starr singing 'Wheel of Fortune' on Radio Luxembourg.

Call-up came for me in May 1953. Just one month after my 18th birthday I walked into the Royal Navy's Victoria Barracks in Portsmouth to become Ordinary Seaman Jackman – service number PJ925695 – sir! I have never forgotten it, and if you were to cut me open, I am convinced you would still find that number imprinted through my torso from end to end, like letters in a stick of rock.

National service was always a lottery. One of my friends, fired up with dreams of becoming a fighter pilot, joined the RAF and spent most of his time building packing cases in Lytham St Annes. As for me, I joined the navy to see the world and ended up onboard a fishery protection minesweeper in Invergordon (more of which later). Yet thousands did manage to serve abroad. Some were given postings to glamorous spots such as Bermuda or the Bahamas, but there was also a real chance of being killed in action in a decade scarred by all kinds of nasty but limited conflicts. One of my friends fought in Korea in 1950. Others tracked down EOKA gunmen in Cyprus or ambushed the Mau Mau gangs in Kenya, but only one came to grief, a former football teammate who was shot in the thigh by communist terrorists while serving as a dog handler with the army in Malaya.

Even for the great majority who never saw action, it was a traumatic experience. Press-ganged from a sheltered life in 'Civvy Street', we were pitchforked into the hurly-burly of service routine with its parade-ground 'bull' and passion for discipline, its strange jargon and spells of frantic activity interspersed with periods of interminable boredom – all for the princely sum of four shillings a day.

Until I joined up, like most young men of my age, I had lived at home. Three weeks later, squeezed uncomfortably into my matelot's blue serge bell-bottomed suit, I was saluting the Queen from the flight deck of the aircraft carrier HMS *Indefatigable* in the Royal Fleet Review at Spithead.

Any romantic notions I might have held about joining the Queen's navy were quickly shattered on my first day. Swift indeed was the transition from civilian to serviceman. First the queue outside the medical orderly's HQ, waiting with sleeves rolled up to receive jabs; then the regulation short-back-and-sides haircut followed by being kitted out with a bewildering array of unfamiliar items – white front, sailor's collar, lanyard, black silk, a sailor's hat with an HMS hatband, navy-blue sweater and two sets of bell-bottoms, all of which had to be stuffed into a kitbag and hauled off to the bleak interior of Victoria Barracks, where I was to spend my first two weeks.

For me and most of my fellow conscripts, national service represented the first taste of the world outside the steadying influence of home. Cut loose from the restraints of family life, it offered wider opportunities for the pursuit of sex. Recruits were warned of the dangers and I well remember watching the medical film, shot in vivid technicolour, with the camera lingering in hideous close-up detail on what you could expect should you contract venereal disease – known in the navy as 'catching the boat up'.

As a teenager my knowledge of sex was founded on little more than smutty jokes and the front covers of *Health & Efficiency* magazine, which always sported a photograph of a bare-breasted woman. As for girls, having been educated in a boys-only grammar school, all I knew was that they were the ones who danced backwards.

I was still a virgin when I joined the navy and listened with growing incredulity to the lurid sexual adventures of my fellow conscripts, several of whom were now expert practitioners in the arcane mysteries of seduction. When writing home to their girlfriends, they would frequently inscribe coded messages on the back of the envelopes, such as 'BURMA' (be undressed ready my angel) or even more explicitly 'NORWICH' (knickers off ready when I come home). One lad from the Isle of Man proudly showed us the love letters he received from his sweetheart adorned with dark curls of her pubic hair.

It was not until midway through national service that my own loss of virginity occurred. I was home on summer leave and travelling down to Cornwall by train with my parents when I got talking to a stunningly attractive girl in the same carriage. To my delight I discovered that she lived only a mile or two from me and, having exchanged addresses, we arranged to meet.

Back home after my holiday I called at her house to suggest an evening at the cinema, hoping at the very least for a snog in the back row as was customary at that time. Instead, to my surprise she proposed a walk in the park, although any romantic intentions I might have harboured were soon dampened when she told me she was a Sunday school teacher.

Nevertheless, we found a park bench and sat down in the dark. She was two years older than me, I discovered, and clearly far more experienced. Before I knew it, I felt her fingers expertly unbuckling my belt. What followed next was over almost before it had begun, but at least I had broken my duck.

Although national service produced the first awakenings of the sexual revolution that would sweep across Britain in the 1960s, other facts of life remained much the same. Few families could afford a car – including mine. Most people still spent their holidays beside the British seaside and the cinema remained the most popular form of entertainment, although trad jazz was beginning to attract a growing cult of duffel-coated fans.

My fellow recruits came from all walks of life and every corner of the country – Geordies, Scousers, Mancs, Brummies, Glaswegians and cockneys – and to be surrounded by so many different accents was a revelation. Invariably, the most easy-going individuals came from rural backgrounds, identified either by the lazy drawl of East Anglia or the rich, rolling burr of the West Country.

Among them was Max Seaford, a bank clerk from Yeovil whose endless repertoire of dirty jokes, told after lights out in a Somerset accent as warm as mulled cider, greatly helped to ease the hardship of those early days. He quickly became the barrack-room comic and, although I did not know it at the time, was destined to have a profound influence on my life.

My stay at Victoria Barracks lasted no more than a fortnight, during which time we were given baseball bats and ordered to patrol the perimeter at night in case of terrorist attacks by the IRA. At that time, I had no idea who or what the IRA was, and what use I might have been in defending the Queen's navy with a baseball bat did not bear thinking about.

The following week we were marched through the dockyard to join HMS *Indefatigable* – an Implacable-class aircraft carrier built by John Brown's shipyard on Clydebank and completed in 1942. She later joined the British Pacific Fleet where, in April 1945, she was struck by a Japanese kamikaze fighter plane carrying a 550-pound bomb. It blasted a gaping hole in her island superstructure but failed to penetrate her armour-plated deck.

She was to be my home for the next 12 weeks of basic training, which was basically a crash course in life below decks. It started early every morning when we were awoken in our hammocks by the bugle blasts of reveille broadcast over the ship's tannoy system, followed by the voice of a duty petty officer bellowing what was to become an all-too-familiar daily litany: '*Heave-ho-heave-ho, lash up and stow; we're off the coast of Spain, there is no sign of rain; leap out, leap out, don't let the sun scorch your bloodshot eyes out!*'

Hardly had I learned how to iron my new navy bell-bottoms (seven creases – one each for the seven seas) than we dropped anchor off Spithead to participate in the Royal Fleet Review. The occasion for putting on this impressive display of Britain's naval sea power was the coronation of Queen Elizabeth II, which had taken place 13 days earlier.

More than 300 ships were involved, lined up in long rows to be formally inspected by the Queen, a custom dating back to 1415 when Henry V reviewed his fleet of a hundred ships at the start of the Hundred Years' War.

We were anchored among eight other aircraft carriers, all in line astern with HMS *Vanguard*, Britain's biggest battleship, at their head, and when the Queen passed by on-board the Royal Yacht, we waved our hats three times above our heads as ordered, having been specifically told to shout 'Hip-hip-hurrah' and not 'hurray!' Never again would Britain put on such a massive display of sea power. Later that night the entire fleet was lit up and the evening ended with a spectacular fireworks display – in all, quite a memorable way to begin my two years before the mast.

Next day we left Spithead, sailing west on a round-Britain cruise that would last the rest of the summer, setting eyes on the Dorset coast and its yellow sandstone cliffs for the first time without knowing how much of my life would take place there.

Our first port of call was Brodick on Arran, where a hike had been planned to climb Goatfell, the island's highest peak. At 2,868 feet (874 metres) above sea level, its granite summit is just 132 feet short of a Munro, but it still represented a strenuous challenge. Wearing oilskins and gaiters, we set off through the murk on a day Scots would describe as *dreich*, with drizzle in the air and the mountain disappearing in the clouds above us. Luckily perhaps, I never reached the top as one of our party broke an ankle and had to be carried back to the ship on a makeshift stretcher, with me taking turns as a stretcher-bearer.

Goatfell was arduous but nothing compared to the night manoeuvres arranged for our stay in Orkney. We had anchored in Scapa Flow, the vast natural harbour at the centre of the archipelago which had become the graveyard of Germany's High Seas Fleet after the First World War, when more than 50 of its ships were scuttled and sent to the bottom.

Put ashore at Moaness Pier on the east coast of Hoy, our objective was to march inland and prevent an opposition force of Royal Marines from sneaking through our lines. Bizarrely, to keep us going we were each given a tin of peaches as iron rations before setting off into the island's treeless hinterland, squelching across endless acres of peatbogs.

By the time we reached our positions it was nearly midnight and the landscape lay bathed in an eerie half-light, a phenomenon known as the 'simmer dim' in the northern isles, when only a few hours of darkness separate the long summer days. For the next hour or two I lay in the heather and ate my tinned peaches as Manx shearwaters flitted past like souls, uttering their unearthly wailing cries in the windless dusk.

It soon became apparent that we had failed utterly to prevent the opposition from crossing the island as we never spotted a single Marine, and the order was given to return to the ship. Already exhausted by the long walk from Moaness, we now began a forced march back to the landing place on blistered feet unused to our unyielding black leather boots.

Mutterings of dissent arose from the ranks. 'What are we doing here?' grumbled one of the regulars from the ship's company. 'I thought we were supposed to be matelots, not bloody soldiers.' Higher up the line, in a vain attempt to raise morale, an officer began to sing in a fine baritone voice: '*Daisy, Daisy, give me your answer, do.*'

'Come on, men,' he entreated, 'surely you know "Daisy"?' But the only response was the sullen tramp of our boots on the road and our mood was far better summed up by the words of 'Bloody Orkney', a poem written by a disenchanted sailor pining for home during the Second World War:

No bloody sport, no bloody games,
No bloody fun the bloody dames
Won't even give their bloody names
In bloody Orkney.

There's nothing greets your bloody eye
But bloody sea and bloody sky,
Roll on demob! We bloody cry
In bloody Orkney.

From Bloody Orkney we completed our round-Britain cruise, learning the difference between a reef knot and a sheet bend, playing basketball in the aircraft hangars, and mastering how to walk in a steady line from one end of the ship to the other without staggering about like a drunk as she rose and fell on the North Sea swell. In short, we were slowly finding our sea legs and becoming real sailors, and on return to Portsmouth, having completed my training I was detailed to join HMS Welcome as a working member of her crew.

Joining *Welcome* was not a case of love at first sight. Launched in 1944, she was an Algerine-class minesweeper, undergoing a refit and propped up in a scruffy Portsmouth dry dock when I found her.

Before heading north to Invergordon, our home base for the next 18 months, we had to carry out sea trials, including the measured mile in the Solent, during which time I was violently seasick. It did not bode well for the future, but miraculously I was never ill again – not even when, years later, I sailed around Land's End aboard a square-rigger in a howling gale.

This was my first real taste of life as part of a ship's company, and by the time we reached Invergordon I had settled down to the crew's watch-keeping routine and canteen-messing system, in which each mess was given an allowance to buy food from the ship's purser, organise its own menus and arrange a rota whereby two men from each mess would prepare the food for the ship's chef to cook in the galley.

By now I was also well versed in the shipboard slang and countless euphemisms employed by generations of Royal Naval matelots down the ages. Thus, Portsmouth was always known as 'Pompey', and Plymouth was 'Jago's Mansions'. Even the navy itself was known mysteriously as 'The Andrew', and the sea was always referred to as 'the oggin'.

In warship terms HMS *Welcome* was a bit of a titch, a mere 225 feet in length with a pugnacious little four-inch anti-aircraft gun up for'ard and a pair of Bofors mounted amidships. Somehow, a ship's company of some 85 officers and ratings were crammed in below decks, and not even her greatest admirers would have called her beautiful; but she was extremely seaworthy, and her modest size enabled us to visit Scottish ports and harbours that larger vessels could not enter.

As for my shipmates, four of them were national servicemen, and as such we tended to bond together, becoming 'oppos' (opposite numbers or best mates). The rest were regulars, tough and hard-bitten individuals who had signed on for eight or twelve years and were able to drink prodigious quantities of beer on their runs ashore. They rightly regarded us as part-time sailors still wet behind the ears, but we nevertheless developed a solid camaraderie.

With them we kept watch, slung our hammocks every evening, rigorously scrubbed ourselves and our clothes in the showers (cleanliness being an essential part of shipboard life in cramped quarters between decks), and learned how to exploit the social division that separated us denizens of the lower decks from our superior officers in the wardroom.

We also discovered the two golden rules that made life more bearable. One was the old sweats' maxim: never volunteer for anything. The other was to master the subtle art of 'skiving' – dodging unpleasant duties by pretending to be busy while doing as little as possible.

Invergordon itself was a revelation. This sleepy village and its natural deepwater port overlooking the Cromarty Firth had been an important base for the Royal Navy in both world wars but was best known for the events that took place in September 1931, when sailors of the Atlantic Fleet mutinied in response to a pay cut ordered by the government of the day. My memories of it revolve mostly around the local hotel that served Scottish high teas by a roaring fire, the skirling of the Invergordon pipe band on practice nights, and the cinema whose tin roof meant that when it rained you could no longer hear the soundtrack.

Even in winter, when the distant summit of Ben Wyvis shone white with snow, the Cromarty Firth lay serene and tranquil. But how different it was when we put to sea. Once we had sailed out between the Sutors of Cromarty – twin headlands like Scylla and Charybdis that acted as the narrow gateway to the Firth – we were at the full mercy of the North Sea gales. Those were the days when submariners received extra pay for spending half their time beneath the sea; and the joke on *Welcome* was that we ought to be paid half as much as them because we used to disappear beneath every other wave.

As 'mess-deck dodger' I had the cushiest job on the ship, scrubbing and polishing down below while my fellow shipmates were exposed to the worst weather Scotland could throw at us.

I loved the Scottish summers and the long, light evenings, listening to Earl Bostic's honking alto saxophone on the ship's radio as we lay at anchor in a moonlit sea loch. Best of all was patrolling in the dog watches when the Hebridean islands were drenched in golden sea light and the gaunt summits of Wester Ross – Beinn Eighe, Stac Pollaidh, Slioch and the rest – stood out against a cloudless sky.

Other times were less benign – such as the night we encountered a vicious storm in the Minch. I was on the bridge as bo'sun's mate in the middle watch, and even the captain looked concerned as we watched the white crests of breaking waves bearing down on us out of the darkness from what seemed a height twice as great as our own.

Watch completed, I went below and crawled into my hammock. When I awoke four hours later the ship lay still and sunlight was streaming in through the open portholes.

While I had been asleep the storm had raced on and we had found shelter in a west coast inlet.

On another occasion I was on duty watch again on a wild night when the officer of the watch called down from the bridge: 'Bo'sun's Mate – bring me a bucket.' Straight away I did as I was bid. 'What do you need the bucket for, sir?' I asked. 'To put some chips in it,' he replied. 'Chips – what chips?' I inquired. 'These,' he answered, and promptly vomited into the bucket.

One of our main tasks as part of the Fishery Protection Squadron was to apprehend any foreign boats fishing in Britain's territorial waters; but with a top speed of 16.5 knots, we only ever managed to catch one hapless Belgian trawler. Instead, most of our time was spent in courtesy calls at little harbours such as Banff and Lossiemouth, dancing eightsome reels in Lerwick with thigh-booted trawlermen, and long days at sea, blowing up halibut with depth charges on anti-submarine exercises.

One of our regular ports of call was Leith, lying in the shadow of the Forth Bridge. At the weekends, after the officers had inspected the mess deck on their regular Saturday morning rounds, the old sweats would head for Fairley's Dancehall in Leith Street and end up getting completely legless; but I used to go into Edinburgh and take one of the city's green trams to the ice rink at Corstophine in the hope of meeting the pretty girl skaters who gathered there.

As well as sleeping in a hammock, which I found extremely comfortable, navy life in the 1950s still clung to other Nelsonian traditions, notably the daily dispensation of rum rations. Every morning the bo'sun's pipe would shrill over the tannoy, followed by the eagerly awaited announcement calling leading hands of the mess for grog. Since I was not yet 20, I was unable to draw my tot. To be listed as teetotal was no hardship as I never liked the stuff anyway, but the older hands would sell their souls for an extra drop. Although forbidden, this could be freely handed over for favours given. The bigger the favour the bigger the drink, ranging from 'sippers' to 'gulpers' and 'see-ers offers' that would render the imbiber legless.

Surprisingly, there was no age barrier regarding tobacco, and although I have always been a devout non-smoker, I happily accepted my monthly gift of 600 cigarettes and the hardened smokers among our ship's company were only too happy to take over my watch-keeping duties in exchange for a month's rations. If we were in Portsmouth this meant I could go 'up the line' to Stoneleigh for the weekend, and one summer I even managed to get home by hitch-hiking all the way from Holyhead.

'Join the navy and see the world' was the slogan that had tempted me. Sadly, apart from the wonders of Scotland's Highlands and islands, my globetrotting was confined to a couple of brief forays across the North Sea. One was to Rotterdam, during which time a coach tour to the Zeedijk, Amsterdam's notorious 'red-light district', provided an education of a completely different kind. The neon-lit brothels and their bare-breasted denizens made Soho look as innocent as a vicar's tea party, and after strolling around for a little while I decided I had seen enough.

Ahead lay a bridge spanning one of the city's canals, and as I began to cross it a dark shadow loomed over me. I looked up and there stood an enormous blonde hooker, at least one foot taller than me. 'Hello darling,' she purred in a rich contralto voice. 'Would you like a f***?' Muttering something like 'that's the last thing on my mind', I sidled past her considerable bulk and scampered back to the safety of the coach.

My only other overseas visit was to Esjberg in Denmark, where we were each given a single Durex condom and lectured by the first lieutenant on the perils of casual sex. 'Remember men,' he cried as we trooped eagerly ashore down the gangplank, 'VD is rife!'

It was not long after this incident that he suffered a mental breakdown and was packed off to Haslar Hospital in Gosport. Our 'Jimmie the One', as all first lieutenants are known in the navy, had never been popular with the ship's company. An extreme disciplinarian, he had soon incurred the displeasure of the older hands, and ever since one of them had hung an imitation noose on his cabin door he had slept with a loaded revolver under his pillow lest he should be hauled out at night and thrown over the side.

At the end of my 18-month stint with the Fishery Protection Squadron, having bid farewell to my shipmates and returned to Portsmouth to be demobbed, *Welcome* had spent more days at sea than any other ship in the Home Fleet.

My last few weeks of national service were spent in Portsmouth Harbour on board HMS *Liverpool*. She was a Town-class light cruiser, a sister ship of HMS *Belfast*, now permanently moored as a museum ship on the Thames in London. In 1943 she took part in the action in which the mighty German warship *Scharnhorst* was sunk, and later survived a serious attack by Italian torpedo bombers in 1942. When the war was over, she returned to Portsmouth to become a floating barracks, an ignominious end for such a doughty old warrior.

It was here while waiting for demob that I learned to type. One day, skiving off from tedious duties such as sweeping the decks or painting the ship's side, I went below and discovered a deserted office with an empty desk and a typewriter on it. Nobody ever found my hideout, and there I shut myself away for hours, emerging only for a mid-morning cuppa when the command for 'stand easy' interrupted my concentration as I slowly mastered the keyboard.

How ironic that after two years being taught how to defend the Queen's realm by firing a Bofors anti-aircraft gun and releasing depth charges, the greatest skill I learned in the navy was my proficiency with a typewriter. I did not know it then, but it would stand me in good stead in the years to come.

Sometimes, looking out from the bridge in the middle watch as *Welcome* rose and fell to the restless rhythm of the North Sea, it seemed as if demob would never come. But when at last I was released back into freedom, I realised that national service had given me a degree of self-reliance and personal pride I had never possessed before. You could always tell those who had done their national service and those who had not. In short, it had made a man of me, although there was still a long way to go until I felt truly grown up.

CHAPTER ELEVEN

ON returning to Civvy Street there seemed no alternative but to resume my dead-end career at Leonard Hill's. Little had changed in my absence and Leonard Hill himself still ruled his empire like a medieval warlord. The overwhelming mood of fear and tedium was relieved only by the companionship of my fellow trainees including Ron Lawrence, who commuted to London from Southend and spent his summer holidays travelling across Spain by motorbike.

Possibly it was the stories of his adventures in Spain that awakened my desire to see the country for myself. So, in 1956 at the age of 21, I persuaded my cousin Peter to accompany me on what would be our first totally independent foreign holiday.

Our destination was the Costa Brava, chosen as much as anything because of its romantic name. More than a hundred years have passed since Ferran Agulló, a Girona-born journalist, first coined the term to describe the cliffs and harbours and pine-fringed coves of northern Catalonia. Since then, much of it has been changed almost out of recognition by the arrival of mass tourism in the 1960s. Norman Lewis, the greatest travel writer of his time, came to the Costa Brava in the late 1940s and his book, *Voices of the Old Sea*, is a perfect freeze-frame evocation of the lives of its inhabitants before the tourist boom.

Having travelled overnight by rail from Paris to Barcelona we arrived in Figueras on a Sunday morning and made our way to the main square, from which buses made their way down to the fishing port of Rosas, some 30 minutes away. The sunlit square was utterly deserted, and as we waited by the bus stop, we heard the clatter of hoofs growing louder by the minute.

Suddenly, from out of a side street a rider emerged astride a white horse and cantered across the heart of the square before disappearing into another street on the other side. As the sound of his hoof-beats was swallowed up and silence returned, we stood for a while without speaking, trying to make sense of what we had seen. Nothing like this ever happened in suburban Surrey, and even before we had reached the Costa Brava, I knew I was going to like it.

When at last the bus arrived it was full of jolly countrywomen, most of them dressed in black with baskets of chickens and apricots on their laps. Sunday was market day in Rosas, and this was obviously a regular outing.

As we set off the clear notes of a guitar rang out from somewhere behind us, cutting through the incomprehensible chatter in raucous Spanish, and suddenly everyone was singing and clapping in time. It was almost too theatrical to be true, and if anyone had tried to organise an introduction to Spain and its exuberant lust for life, they could not have done better.

Before I knew it, someone was handing me a *porrón*, a leather wineskin from which you drink by holding it at arm's length and squirting the contents down your throat. The wine was delicious, my first-ever taste, rough and red and ideal for the occasion. How they laughed as I spilled half of it down my shirt; but I did not care. As if taking part in an impromptu fiesta, we bowled down to the coast in party mood to the foot-stamping rhythm of our fellow passengers with the windows wide open and even the driver singing at the wheel as the roadside plane trees went swishing past, arriving in Rosas just as the fishing fleet was returning.

Rosas turned out to be an inspired choice, its buildings bleached as white as bones cast up on the rim of a turquoise bay. For much of the day the town lay silent, as if drugged by sunlight, while its inhabitants took their *siestas* behind beaded doorways. Apart from a solitary member of the Guardia Civil lounging outside the police post in his tricorn hat and sinister sunglasses, it seemed almost deserted until the heavy pulse of ships' engines announced the return of the fishing boats in late afternoon.

This was the signal for everyone to gather by the quayside to watch the day's catch being unloaded. Nothing I had ever seen in Cornwall could surpass the bounty laid out for auction on wickerwork platters: skate and dogfish still feebly flapping, red mullet with scales the size of thumbnails, spiny lobsters, glutinous piles of baby octopus and a moray eel as thick as my thigh.

Later that evening at our little seafront *hostal* we met the only other Englishman staying in Rosas. During our conversation over dinner, I made an innocent comment about the framed photos of General Franco who stared down at us from every wall. At once there was a sudden clatter of cutlery being laid down, followed by an awkward silence as everyone turned around to face us. 'Mention not the name,' hissed our English friend as life in the room went back to normal. 'It just isn't done.' Clearly, Franco's loathsome fascist regime still had the power to supress its people.

This was the only shadow on our idyllic surroundings, and in the evenings, feeling terribly grown-up, we would stroll along the waterfront and order a liqueur, a glass of *Aromas de Montserrat* from the famous monastery near Barcelona, while nightingales sang in the overgrown ruins of the 11th-century Ciutadella and hawk moths attracted by tubs of night-scented flowers whirred blindly around the café tables.

My cousin Peter was the ideal companion for such an adventure. He had inherited his father's sense of humour and shared my love of the natural world, although even then we viewed it in a different light. Already he was beginning to take a more scientific approach, while I remained an incurable romantic, which is why I went on to be a writer and Peter would later become a professor at Princeton University, renowned for his life's work studying Darwin's finches in the Galapagos.

We spent the days swimming in rock-bound coves, chasing swallowtail butterflies and listening to the hoopoes – candy-pink birds as delicate as porcelain with ornate crests and woodwind voices – softly repeating their name in the olive groves. By the end of the week, we could hardly bear to tear ourselves away, and I knew then, no matter what course my life would take, that travelling would be a part of it.

Back in London I resumed my treadmill existence, commuting each day to Leonard Hill's new premises in Eden Street, a grubby cul-de-sac off Tottenham Court Road which seemed like the perfect metaphor to describe my dead-end job.

Two year later I was still there. It was now 1958, when a pint of beer cost one-and-sixpence and I knew that petrol was two shillings a gallon – even though I did not have a car at that time.

This was the year in which half the Manchester United football team was killed in a plane crash. The London Planetarium opened and so did Gatwick Airport. Work on the M1 – Britain's first motorway – began. Britain's first parking meters were installed. Sandi Toksvig was born, and Ralph Vaughan Williams died.

It was also the year of Teddy boys with drainpipe trousers and 'duck's arse' haircuts; when our pin-ups were Brigitte Bardot,

Marilyn Monroe and Sophia Loren; and our idea of a big night out was snogging in the back row of the Odeon in North Cheam while Kirk Douglas was starring in *The Vikings*.

As for popular music, the choice lay between Johnnie Ray and Frankie Laine, Mantovani's Orchestra, and the Billy Cotton Band Show. Then suddenly, into this cultural wasteland came two events that would transform our humdrum post-war existence. One was the arrival of coffee bars – whose exotic décor of rubber plants and bamboo furniture hinted at a world infinitely more exciting than Sutton High Street on a wet Saturday.

The other was skiffle – a DIY musical phenomenon born in the intervals at Chris Barber's Jazz Club and brought to the ears of the public by Lonnie Donegan's nasal twang as he sang about the 'Rock Island Line'. Almost overnight the craze caught on and took root in the steamy interiors of coffee bars up and down the land – the most famous being the 2i's in Old Compton Street, Soho, run by an Australian ex-wrestler called Paul Lincoln who used to fight under the name of 'Doctor Death'.

One evening, with my fellow Eden Street slaves Bob Jones, Ron Lawrence and John Willard, we paid our admission fee and went downstairs into the smoke-filled dive at the 2i's and listened to Wally Whyton and the Vipers Skiffle Group singing 'Don't You Rock Me Daddy-O'.

We were hooked on the spot. Ron, who could already play the guitar, showed me the 'three-chord trick' that could be used to accompany almost any song. Then all we needed was a rhythm section: a tea-chest bass and a washboard plus an eclectic repertoire of hot gospel, Delta blues, Hank Williams' country music and Woody Guthrie's Dustbowl Ballads – and the Eden Street Skiffle Group was born.

It was at this point that Hamish Maxwell entered my life. The introduction came about through Mickey Hopkins, a friend of mine who belonged to the same football club as me. He also played mandolin for a local skiffle group out in the *banlieues* of Mitcham and Morden and suggested I should listen to them. Hamish was their lead singer, and it was not long before I persuaded them both to jump ship and join the Eden Street Skiffle Group.

With his big voice and Gibson guitar we really took off. We did half a dozen gigs on the radio, played at the Royal Festival Hall and the Albert Hall, cut a plastic record that still sells at silly prices on eBay and appeared on the BBC's popular *Six-Five Special*.

We also became the resident band at the Skiffle Cellar, a bohemian dive in Greek Street, run by Russell Quaye, a red-bearded busker and wartime rear gunner, and his wife, Hylda Sims, a folk singer, writer, poet, and teacher. Together they performed as the City Ramblers and like them, we played there every week alongside celebrities such as Chas McDevitt, Ramblin' Jack Elliott and American bluesmen like Sonny Terry and Brownie McGhee before hurrying off at the end of the evening, still smelling of stale sweat and tobacco, to catch the last train home to Stoneleigh.

By now we had become such regular Soho denizens that even the raddled old hookers would no longer sidle up and whisper 'Fancy a good time, dearie?' as we walked past with our guitar cases to meet up for a pint at the Pillars of Hercules or eat gargantuan plates of wurst and sauerkraut at Madame Maurer's, Hamish's favourite London restaurant with its zinc bar and blue plastic cow in the window.

When I first knew Hamish, he was the uncrowned King of Sutton. Outrageously good-looking with his neatly trimmed beard and twinkling brown eyes, he strolled up and down the High Street in a green tartan suit, complete with a yellow rose in his buttonhole and a walking stick with a dog's-head handle. The girls adored him, and nobody who saw him in all his finery would have believed he was a chef, working in the bowels of the Cock Hotel with a roguish lad called Reg.

In no time our lives became entwined, first at the all-night parties we used to attend in Sutton on most weekends, and later with hilarious tea parties at Hamish's house, where his mother prepared endless plates of toasted teacakes and looked on in bewilderment at the odd assortment of ravenous friends who fell about laughing and cracked risqué jokes she mercifully never understood.

On Sunday nights, suitably attired in jumbo cords and desert boots, we would meet at the Queen Vic Jazz Club and listen to the Mike Daniels Delta Jazzmen, howling with testosterone-fuelled longing as Doreen Beatty, almost spilling out of her skintight green silk sheath dress, rubbed herself suggestively against the microphone as she sang 'Gimme a Pigfoot and a Bottle of Beer'.

One of my closest friends at that time was Ian Stewart, a big-hearted Scotsman from Pittenweem on the coast of Fife, with piercing blue eyes, a prominent chin, and a randy girlfriend. Even then, he was a talented boogie piano player and regularly performed on stage during the intervals at the Queen Vic, and it came as no surprise when he later became a founding member of the Rolling Stones, who I used to follow at the Station Hotel in Richmond long before they became world-famous.

CHAPTER TWELVE

IT was around this time that I experienced another of those unexpected sea changes that completely altered the direction of my life. Not long after leaving the navy I hitchhiked down to Yeovil to meet up with Max Seaford, my old shipmate while training on board HMS *Indefatigable*. When I rang the bell at his house, his mother came to the door. 'Where's Max?' I asked. 'He's gone to West Bay,' she said, a place I had never heard of on the Dorset coast. Foolishly, I had never told him I was coming. I just assumed he would be at home.

He had some friends who lived in a block of flats called Pier Terrace, said his mother, and there was a bus that would take me as far as Bridport, from where I could walk the last mile or so down to West Bay.

This part of the West Country was completely new to me and the countryside was a revelation. Beyond Beaminster the road wound in sinuous curves through the green hills of Dorset. It was May, and the sun was shining on old-fashioned meadows bright with buttercups. The roadsides were buried in a froth of cow parsley and I thought I had never seen anywhere quite so quintessentially English.

At first sight I found West Bay rather disappointing. Perhaps I had expected something more picturesque, like Polperro, or Port Isaac. Instead, it was simply a workaday harbour wedged between corrugated yellow sandstone cliffs at the easternmost end of

Chesil Beach. Joan of Navarre had arrived here in 1403 on her way to marry Henry IV. Otherwise, history had totally passed it by.

At least Pier Terrace was easy to find; a Flemish-style, four-storey block of flats, completed in 1886 alongside the east pier two years after the arrival of the Great Western Railway. The locals never thought much of it and dubbed it Noah's Ark.

At the entrance was a note pinned beside the doorbell. 'This is the abode of Roger Courtney and Bill Snakebite Hitchcock,' it read. 'Friends ring twice. Girls come straight up.' I rang the bell and climbed upstairs as directed to an attic on the top floor. The door was open and from inside came the sound of voices singing a popular West Country anthem:

Half a pound of flour and lard makes lovely clacker[1],
Some for thee and some for I, cor bugger Janner.
Oh! How happy us'll be when we get back to the West Country,
Where the oggies[2] grow on trees, cor bugger Janner.

For a moment I stood in the doorway. There stood Max, larger than life as ever, surrounded by the girls who had walked straight up, and his friends who would also become mine. 'Jacko!' he cried. 'What the bloody hell are you doing here?' Then, after shaking hands with all his pals, we all went out to celebrate our reunion in The Bridport Arms.

Such was my introduction to the simple pleasures of West Bay: drinking snakebite (a vile but cheap concoction of rough cider

---

[1]clacker = pastry

[2]oggies = Cornish pasties

mixed with blackcurrant cordial to take the taste away), swimming between the twin stone piers that formed the harbour entrance and sunbathing on the East Beach before heading off to an all-night party somewhere in the hinterland.

By the end of the weekend, I had not only renewed the bonds of friendship with my old *Indefatigable* oppo, but also made what would turn out to be a host of new friends whose companionship would last a lifetime. Louis and Val Elliot, Guy and Gill Grafton, Aly Pritchard, Eric Hamblett and Geoff Manley are names that will mean nothing to the casual reader but still resonate with me.

Also among them were Ray Harvey and Eva, his girlfriend who was soon to become his wife. Ray was a true countryman, heavily built and easy-going with a deep-down Dorset accent, and Eva was a raven-haired beauty with huge brown eyes and a smile that would melt an iceberg.

After they were married, they bought a cottage in Corscombe, midway between Bridport and Yeovil, and I painted a mural of Chinese goldfish on their bathroom wall. Where a stream flowed through the bottom of their garden stood a dilapidated caravan made from the plywood fuselage of a wartime glider, and on subsequent visits it became my weekend hideaway. As a bedroom it was basic in the extreme but perfectly adequate for my needs. Once, arriving late on a Friday night as usual, I found that mice had made their nest in a pair of trousers I had left behind.

Wrapped in Corscombe's rural hush I fell asleep to the sound of the stream trickling past on its way to Sutton Bingham reservoir, and in the mornings, after joining Ray and Eva for a monumental breakfast of bacon and eggs, we would all pile into their Land Rover and head down to West Bay.

It was skiffle that really helped to cement our friendship. Impressed by the fact that the Eden Street Skiffle Group had become well known on the London folk-club scene I suggested that we should all descend on West Bay for a weekend of music and general debauchery.

Our first gig was in George's, the now defunct Bridport bakery in East Street, where we teamed up with the local Hemp City Skiffle Group and learned some of their bawdy Dorset repertoire, including a particular favourite called 'The Thrashing Machine'. The evening was a huge success, and the West Dorset magic became all-powerful, not just for me but for Ian Stewart and some of my other Surrey friends, too.

We were Sutton twinned with West Bay and became regular visitors, squashed into Hamish's purple-painted Austin Heavy Twelve, which sometimes managed to travel as far as Winchester without getting a puncture. Eventually the pull became so great that some of the Surrey Chapter – Hamish included – migrated to West Bay for good.

Those idyllic Wessex summers were among the most carefree times of my life. Escaping from London on a Friday evening, going west with the light, we ate our ham-and-pickle sandwiches as we followed the sun across the New Forest, keeping our eyes peeled for the wild ponies that sometimes strayed across the road and caused horrific accidents. The car radio was always switched on, and it was on one such journey in July 1961 I heard the news that Ernest Hemingway, one of my literary heroes, had committed suicide at his home in Ketchum, Idaho.

Like migrating swallows, we returned to Dorset every summer to renew our friendships and make new ones. Among them was Arthur Watson, whom I met one night, cooking mackerel over a driftwood fire on the Chesil Beach, and who went on to open a famous seafood restaurant in West Bay.

It was around this time that I also got to know two of the local fishermen, Rex Woolmington and Barry Hawker, co-owners of the *Peace and Plenty*, an old-time Cornish pilchard lugger with a small wheelhouse aft and a rust-red retainer sail.

Rex had the broadest Dorset accent I had ever heard, and Barry was blessed with a piratical face straight out of central casting. Together they were tremendous fun. With them the banter never stopped, and when they put to sea, I would accompany them as an unpaid deckhand, laying down crab pots, taking angling parties mackerel fishing and setting trammel nets for what Rex called 'they gurt shiners', as salmon were known.

We were not the only summer visitors. Every year saw an influx of extremely attractive French girls who attended a secretarial course in Bridport. Inevitably, we were drawn to each other and various romances blossomed, including one between me and a gamine young Parisienne called Claude.

For some reason I could never fathom, Claude and her fellow students found it highly amusing that we always greeted each other in typical broad Dorset style: 'Mornin' my flower,' someone would say, and it was not long before they began to refer to us collectively as The Flowers. The name stuck. We were the West Bay Flowers for evermore, and Ray and Eva Harvey even named their cottage *Mosfas*, an anacronym for Members of the Senior Flowers Association.

One year a German coaster called the *Visurgis* became a regular visitor in the harbour, bringing timber from the Baltic and returning home via Teignmouth with a cargo of china clay. We became friends with Horst, the skipper, and one day he invited us to sail with him down to Teignmouth.

We put to sea on one of those golden midsummer evenings with not a breath of wind and the water like a mirror. Eventually the moon rose, laying a silver path across Lyme Bay as Claude and I sat on the bridge, arms around each other's shoulders, drinking lager into the small hours as the red cliffs of south Devon slid past on the starboard side, until all too soon it was time to go ashore in Teignmouth and hitchhike back to West Bay.

When September came and the sprat shoals arrived like dark clouds off Chesil Beach, Claude returned to Paris. The summer was over, and I was about to encounter another of those milestone moments when the compass turned in a completely new direction.

PART TWO

TO AFRICA
AND BEYOND

'To love a place truly you must know it in all its seasons.'
From *Wild About Britain* (Bradt, 2014)

CHAPTER THIRTEEN

IN my mid-twenties, for the first time in my life, I was sacked after Leonard Hill realised that I was never going to make him a fortune selling advertising space for the *Muck Shifter*. After the initial indignity of being fired, I felt that a huge weight had been lifted from my shoulders. Within days I found another job with an advertising agency, during which time I happened to see an ad in the 'situations vacant' columns of *Advertising Weekly*.

'Wanted: copywriter for Poly Travel', it read. They were looking for someone to write deathless prose about sun-kissed beaches for their holiday brochures. On a whim, I applied for it, even though I had absolutely no experience as a copywriter, so you can imagine my surprise when I got the job.

My new boss was Peter Gibson, and he was a joy to work for. Although not much older than me he was articulate, well educated, and highly sophisticated. Just why he chose to employ me – a rank beginner – I will never know; but after a whistle-stop tour around Europe looking at the tourist resorts that I was supposed to write up, I survived.

I had been with Poly Travel for about a year when I met Ted Appleton, who was employed in the accounts department but also worked as a travel writer in his spare time. This I discovered as we were leaving the office one day and I noticed he was carrying a suitcase. 'Going somewhere nice?' I asked him. 'The Cinque Terra,' he replied. 'I'm going to write a travel article about it for *Woman's Own*.'

'You mean they actually give you a free holiday?' I asked incredulously. 'It's better than that,' he said. 'They also pay you for the story.' It sounded almost too good to be true, and I knew then what I wanted to do more than anything else on earth.

To achieve my dream took a few more years. By then I had left Poly Travel to work for the British Tourist Authority in their editorial department, based in St James's Street; and I was married and living in a ground-floor bed-sit in Clapham Common.

For a year or so I had been in a relationship with Sarah, a former art student who lived in Surrey and had become part of our Sutton crowd. I was still living at home when my 29th birthday came around and I had never had a steady girlfriend for so long before. 'I suppose we might as well get married,' I suggested one day. 'I suppose we might as well,' she replied.

There was no engagement ring. Instead, I bought her a pair of ski boots and we spent our honeymoon skiing in Austria. Her ski-school teacher had the unfortunate name of Adolf, and one of our fellow guests at our small hotel was a genuine old-style Prussian, complete with sabre scars on both cheeks, who always sliced the top off his boiled egg at breakfast as if decapitating his enemy. We both hoped nobody would realise we were on honeymoon, but as we sat down to join him one morning he rose to his feet, clicked his heels, and said: 'Und how are ze little darlings zis morning?'

We lived in Clapham just long enough to be burgled. Coming home one evening after visiting Sarah's parents, we found one of our ground-floor windows open. Outside on the ground was our portable radio and a few other semi-precious possessions. We must have disturbed the thief just as he was about to leave with his booty.

Indoors by the open window stood a glass carboy in which Sarah had artfully arranged a bunch of dried teasels, and I noticed some strands of wool attached to the prickly seed heads. The burglar must have rubbed against them when making his getaway, and I pointed this out to the plain-clothes police officer who turned up to inspect the crime scene. He turned to me with a withering look. 'You've been reading too many Sexton Blake novels, son,' he said.

For me, living in London was tolerable only because we could escape at weekends to visit Sarah's parents in Little Bookham. They lived in a bungalow with easy access to the loveliest parts of Surrey, and I could not have wished for kinder in-laws, who always welcomed me into their home with unfailing generosity. On Sunday afternoons, accompanied by Sarah's two brothers and sister, we would go for long winter walks in the leafless woods around Shere and Abinger Hatch before ending up with a family tea by the fireside.

Meanwhile, on one of our summer visits to Dorset we had bought a tumbledown cottage for a song – you still could in those days. Even then I was not earning enough to complete the purchase and had to borrow from my father after the bank refused to help, saying they never lent money on old properties – as this one certainly was.

It must once have been a farm labourer's cottage, a tumbledown hulk no bigger than a haystack, built of Hamstone under a thatched roof which had long since fallen in. The living room walls were green with damp after standing empty for several months, and when I went to look at the bedrooms I fell through the stairs, which had rotted away.

But as all estate agents tell you, location is everything, and Way Cottage, as it was called, stood on a hillside in the village of

Powerstock, lost in the hills four miles from Bridport. What I had stumbled on was a backwater on the way to nowhere, hemmed in by lynchets – medieval strip-fields too steep to plough – and threaded by hollow ways so deep in places they almost shut out the sky.

At first it was just a weekend bolthole. As for the village itself, it is pretty but not self-consciously so. There is a pub (Victorian), a castle mound (Saxon) and a real *Cider with Rosie* village school. At its centre where five lanes meet stands the Church of St Mary's with its crooked Norman chancel arch and a gilded weathercock slowly turning in the wind on its yellow Hamstone tower.

The churchyard is an ancient silence of sombre yews and leaning headstones. When I first came to live there it was the abode of Lazarus, a one-eyed tomcat who lived in a sepulchre and emerged at night to make sleep impossible with his amorous yowling.

Those were the days when barn owls hunted over the sloping hay meadows, when colonies of house martins still built their mud nests under the eaves of The Three Horseshoes, and the old men sinking their pints inside spoke with such a broad Dorset burr I could only understand one word in three.

During the week I still had to go back to London; but when Friday came, I could hardly wait to drive westward and eventually leave the A35 to follow the Roman road to Eggardon, the giant hill fort that sits astride the geological frontier where the rolling chalk downs of the south country end and the true West Country begins.

From here it is downhill all the way. As you plunge ever deeper down the burrowing lanes, the landscape changes before your eyes, welcoming you with a flourish of ferns and the unmistakable smell of wild garlic until the village appears in the last of the light.

The change in the landscape is sudden and unmistakable. Gone are the high, bare fields of the open chalklands that line the Roman road from Dorchester. In their place rise the rounded hills of greensand country, separated by a maze of secret valleys and, farther west, the wet clay meadows of the Marshwood Vale lapping around the feet of Pilsdon Pen.

None of it is wild in the sense that Dartmoor or the Lakeland Fells are wild. West Dorset is a softer, altogether friendlier landscape, almost entirely shaped by centuries of human toil. In the valleys around Powerstock and West Milton you can still see the long, thin ridges which are the ghosts of ancient fields.

Here in the mornings, we awoke to the sound of cows being driven down the lane after milking, the soft clatter of hooves and the slap of cowpats hitting the tarmac; and when I looked out of our bedroom window, there stood Eggardon at the head of the valley, a billowing cloud of grassy limestone starred with flocks of grazing sheep.

Upon its summit, 830 feet above the sea, where the skylarks sing among the clouds, nothing changes. 'As old as Eggardon' goes the local saying. Until recently, a solitary thorn tree stood on the top, ringed by ramparts raised in the Iron Age. This wind-bent relic was planted in the 18th century by Isaac Gulliver, known as 'the king of the Dorset smugglers', and was used as a day mark for ships beating into Lyme Bay with contraband cargoes of French silk and brandies, and on a summer evening, when the sea turns to silver and the West Country light is as sharp as cider, you can see as far as Dartmoor.

Confined in the county's westernmost corner, this is what I came to think of as my Dorset. It is certainly not Thomas Hardy's Wessex, still less the genteel world of Jane Austen, and has no official boundaries: only the crumbling Jurassic cliffs, thick with fossils, from Abbotsbury to Lyme Regis. Inland it melts away somewhere just north of Beaminster.

That is the big picture. But the epicentre falls within a five-mile radius of Powerstock. For me this is the magic circle, a rumpled, tumbling green-gold land of secret combes and sensuously rounded plum-pudding hills. In pure landscape terms it is the only part of the British Isles that still reminds me of the lost countryside of my childhood.

CHAPTER FOURTEEN

ALTHOUGH I enjoyed working for the British Travel Association, I had not forgotten Ted Appleton and the lure of travel writing as a career. Eventually, I plucked up courage and sent a couple of unsolicited pieces to the *Daily Telegraph*. To my delight they accepted both for a series on 'Weekends Away'.

Encouraged by my seeing my byline in such a prestigious publication I decided to send a feature to the *Sunday Times*, then generally recognised as the most exciting newspaper in the country. Once more I was thrilled to hear they had accepted my story, and at the same time I also received a letter from Jean Robertson, their distinguished travel editor, inviting me to lunch.

Imagine my surprise when, halfway through the meal, I was offered a job on the paper's travel desk. Two weeks later I was the lowest paid journalist on the *Sunday Times*, but I did not care. It was more money than I had earned before, and better still, it was Harold Evans who had agreed to take me on.

Harold Evans – Harry to everyone on the paper – was a no-nonsense northerner with piercing blue eyes and a small, wiry frame that had earned him the nickname of 'the demon jockey', not only because of his diminutive build but also as a tribute to his restless nature and speed of thought.

Born in 1928, it came as no surprise to me when British journalists voted him the greatest British newspaper editor of all time in 2001, or when he was knighted for his services to his profession three years later.

His meteoric rise to fame was a classic example of meritocracy in action at a time when class and privilege no longer held back men and women of talent.

His father was a train driver, his mother a housewife who ran a grocery shop in Eccles, and both were what Evans describes as 'respectable working class'.

Having left school at 16 he started work as a cub reporter on the Ashton-under-Lyne *Weekly Reporter*. After national service in the RAF, he went on to work at the *Manchester Evening News* before becoming editor of the *Northern Echo* in Darlington at the age of 32. There he quickly acquired his reputation for investigative journalism which, based on his fearless determination to discover the truth, led to his appointment in 1967 as editor of the *Sunday Times*, a job he held until 1981.

Once he got his teeth into a story, he would never let go whatever the risks, and his staff revered him for it. We were all driven on by his unswerving belief that every one of us should work our socks off but have fun doing it. No wonder we became known as 'Harry's Children', and I was hugely proud to be one of them.

I was blessed in having some wonderful colleagues to subedit my copy and guide me safely through my baptism in this hothouse of talent. Among them was Ian Jack, a bespectacled Glaswegian with an addiction to chocolates, who later became the editor of *Granta*, and once complained to me that he was 'Just the middle seven letters of your name.'

As for the rest of my colleagues, they were the most extraordinary collection of individuals ever gathered under one roof. Drawn from all corners of the country, they were united in their passion for journalism. Many were household names such as Michael Parkinson, who worked on the sports pages, and the bubbly haired novelist Jilly Cooper. As for me, the *Sunday Times* became the university I never went to; and thanks to their unstinting kindness and the inspiration they provided, I survived.

****

When I joined the paper in 1970 there was no such thing as wildlife tourism; but already a sea change was taking place in the way the natural world was regarded. It began in 1962 with the publication of *Silent Spring* by the American biologist Rachel Carson. Described as the most important book of the 20th century, this was the catalyst that launched environmentalism, pinpointing the destruction of the delicate balance of nature by the indiscriminate use of pesticides such as DDT, whose insidious presence in Britain brought about the near extinction of such iconic wildlife species as otters and peregrine falcons.

Together with the *Torrey Canyon* oil spill off Land's End in 1967, Carson's book touched a popular nerve. By the time I joined the ranks of Fleet Street the green shoots of environmentalism were breaking out everywhere, yet I was amazed to discover how seldom the subject reached the travel pages. In ecological terms I had found a niche which I could exploit and make my own. I made no secret of my passion for the natural world, and in time the penny dropped. 'Don't send him to Torremolinos,' the travel desk would say. 'It's not his kind of tundra.'

Even so, I was totally unaware that what I was doing was paving the way for ecotourism. Even the word itself was unknown to me, first being coined in 1983 by a Mexican conservationist, Hector Ceballos-Lascurain, to describe nature-based travel to wilderness areas.

For anyone involved with conservation the 1970s was an exciting decade. It was like witnessing the birth of a new religion. Television was paramount in spreading the word, and in 1978 I received a call from David Attenborough who had just been filming mountain gorillas for the BBC's *Life on Earth* series. At that time fewer than 500 of these highly endangered primates lived in the cloudforests of Rwanda's Virunga volcanoes, where Dian Fossey, an American primatologist, had been studying them for several years.

The BBC film was based around Digit, a young male gorilla whose group had become habituated to Dian's presence. Attenborough explained how Digit had been killed by poachers on New Year's Eve and was clearly upset. It was, he said, 'not just the death of an animal but an act of murder.'

In response I flew to Rwanda and wrote up the story of Digit's demise. With the help of the Fauna and Flora Preservation Society, an appeal was launched that soon raised £5,000 for what became the Mountain Gorilla Project.

While rightly revered as the saviour of the species, Dian was a complex and reclusive character and was vehemently opposed to the idea of gorilla tourism. At the time of her death in 1985, poaching had reduced the population to its lowest ebb of around 250 gorillas. Since then, gorilla trekking has become a multi-million-dollar business in which tourists are happy to pay up to $1,500 for the privilege of spending an hour in the close company of these gentle giants.

******

Globetrotting was not my father's strong suit. Although he loved our annual trips to Cornwall, the furthest he had been abroad was a booze cruise to Calais towards the end of his life; yet he had always been an enthusiastic armchair traveller. Seldom a week went by without him bringing home a library book written by African explorers or big-game hunters, which I, too, read avidly, learning the beautiful Swahili names of all the animals – *chui* (leopard), *ndovu* (elephant), and most thrilling of all, *simba* (lion).

Slowly, a picture emerged, of a heat-stunned wilderness of dust and thorns and golden savannahs I longed to visit; but how? Safaris were the domain of the rich and revolved mostly around trophy hunting; yet already the winds of change had begun to blow across that vast, dusty continent. Photo safaris were what people wanted now, and the growth of package holidays combined with the arrival of jumbo jets had made Africa more accessible than ever.

Nevertheless, it remained a dream that lay far beyond anything I could afford – until I joined the *Sunday Times*. Now, as a travel writer there was nowhere so remote or so eye-wateringly expensive that I could not visit in pursuit of a story. Later I would also discover that my new profession was a magic key that unlocked all kinds of secret worlds, in which I would be privileged to spend time with a host of extraordinary characters I would never have met otherwise. And among them were all my heroes, not the football stars whose sublime talents I so envied, but kindred spirits such as Sir Peter Scott and Sir David Attenborough who, like me, were in love with the natural world and driven by an insatiable curiosity to seek it out wherever it existed.

Desperate though I was to visit Africa, safari holidays were still a niche market and my first assignments were closer to home: Cyprus, Spain, and a handful of destinations within Britain, including a memorable walk up the Pennine Way with Reg Hookway, the director of the Countryside Commission.

What made it special was not only the brooding landscapes of the Peak District National Park we encountered as we made our way up the spine of England, but his extraordinary account of his exploits in the Second World War.

At the age of 19 he had been parachuted into Yugoslavia to support Tito's Partisan fighters in their guerrilla war against their Nazi occupiers. 'I don't know why I'm telling you this,' he said as curlews called across the peat hags. 'I've never spoken about it to anyone before.'

Within days of arriving, he had joined a group of Partisans who had laid siege to a village occupied by German troops. Eventually, the soldiers laid down their weapons and emerged, hands in the air, led by an officer waving a white flag. The Partisan leader ordered them to stand in line. 'Is that all of you?' he shouted. The officer nodded, and the Partisans opened fire with their automatic weapons until not a man was left standing.

'I was aghast,' recalled Hookway. 'How could you shoot unarmed men after they had surrendered'? 'We will show you,' replied the Partisan leader, 'then you will never have to ask us again.'

He accompanied them into the mountains and in a little while they reached a deserted village. Some of the houses were still smouldering where they had been burned to the ground. The Germans had been there only a few days ago and massacred every man, woman and child.

Having fought side by side with Tito's guerrillas all through the war, I wondered how he could have ever settled down again when peace was restored. For him, the answer was finding solace in the countryside, walking in the silence of the hills that rose and fell before us on our way to the thundering waters of High Force and the wildflowers of Upper Teesdale.

And then at last, back in the office on my return to London, came the moment I had been waiting for. It was an invitation to join a small press trip to Kenya.

****

Nothing prepares you for the impact of Africa. Strange sights, new sounds, unfamiliar smells. It is a total assault on the senses, like being a child again and seeing the world afresh. Once you have been there, breathed its dry air, watched distant storms trailing across its immense horizons and been awakened by a million purring doves, you will never be the same. At least, despite everything I had read, that is how it was for me.

My initiation took place in Kenya's Masai Mara national reserve. I had flown by light aircraft from Nairobi at the end of the rains and the land was still as green as Ireland as we bounced from one thermal to the next over endless plains on which herds of buffaloes stampeded away beneath our wings.

Even before we touched down on the rough dirt airstrip, I knew it would be love at first sight. The *kiangazi* was just beginning, the dry season that would tempt the migrating wildebeest to pour in from the Serengeti, and the ripening grasses had not yet been reduced to stubble by the hungry herds. Instead, they stood tall, rippling in the wind like the waves of the sea towards a horizon so far away that it seemed like the edge of the world.

Until then I had never seen an elephant in the wild, tusks gleaming, huge ears flapping; six tonnes of silence drifting like smoke between the thorn trees. Nor had I heard the rumble of lions greeting the dawn.

Next morning, I set out at first light to find the cats before they sought the shade and had not gone far when we spotted an adult pride male perched on a termite mound. He was still quite a long way off, so I watched him with my binoculars, a magnificent sight with his mane backlit by the rising sun.

He began to roar through half-closed jaws, and with every cavernous groan his breath condensed in the sharp morning air like smoke from a dragon's nostrils. All other sound ceased, as if the whole world were listening, and the hairs on the back of my neck stood on end and I thought: Who could fail to be hooked on lions after a moment like that?

CHAPTER FIFTEEN

THE 1970s would turn out to be a tumultuous decade for me. Having moved out of the flat in London, Sarah and I were back in Surrey, albeit further out in a Guildford semi, and in 1971 I became the proud father of a baby daughter. We called her Imogen, and I watched her transformation with amazement and delight, from the wrinkled homunculus I had seen within minutes of her birth to an adorable little blue-eyed girl with blond curls and a blessedly placid nature.

Over the next two years, on most Friday evenings we would pack everything into my Sunbeam Alpine sports car – clothes, wellies, frying pan, Lopez the tabby cat and Imogen in her carrycot – and drive down to Dorset for the weekend. Returning to Guildford late on Sunday, I would turn up at work next morning feeling like death warmed up; but fortunately for me, this situation would not last much longer.

In 1970, the same year that I had joined the *Sunday Times*, Kenneth Allsop and his family moved into Milton Mill in the village of West Milton, just a mile down the road from Powerstock. I did not meet him until the following year. Nor did I know then that he would become my mentor and my guru.

Born in Yorkshire in 1920, he was destined to become one of the most versatile journalists of his day; but it was the film-star features and the well-bred voice rather than the omnipresent byline that made Kenneth Allsop a household name when he joined *Tonight*, the BBC's flagship current affairs programme in 1960, and went on to become one of Britain's most widely recognised celebrities as a commentator and acerbic interviewer.

Although best known for his on-screen fame, he always regarded himself first and foremost as a writer, firmly anchored in the print journalism of Fleet Street. He detested the term 'television personality' not only because it overshadowed his reputation as one of Fleet Street's finest but because it also obscured his reputation as an author and his abiding passion for the natural world.

Inspired by the work of nature writers such as W. H. Hudson, Richard Jefferies and Henry Williamson above all others, he was awarded the 1950 John Llewellyn Rhys Prize for his novel, *Adventure Lit Their Star*, but was sidetracked by the allure of Fleet Street and its greater financial rewards.

Arriving at the Mill to meet the great man was like breaking a dream. I realised I had been there before, having been invited to an all-night party back in the 1960s. Friends had driven me there, and having spent the night at this idyllic Georgian mill house, I left next morning none the wiser as to its location deep in the rumpled hills of West Dorset until that first meeting, reminiscent of the lost chateau in Alain Fournier's novel, *Le Grand Meaulnes*.

I found Ken to be the best of company, exuding an aura of warmth that was part of his extraordinary charisma. 'Like standing in front of an open fire,' is how the *Sunday Times* columnist Alan Brien once described it. 'A feeling that spread through the room the moment he came in.'

Although I was in awe of this legendary figure, we struck up an immediate friendship based on our shared interests in journalism, natural history and the burgeoning environmental movement that was just beginning to flex its muscles, and the following year to my great delight we also became colleagues when he joined me at the *Sunday Times* in the summer of 1972.

Inevitably, whenever I called at the Mill, I would find him seated at his typewriter – no computers in those days – in a study lined with books from floor to ceiling. He used to say that he envied my 'untrammelled existence' as a fledgling travel writer. For him, the pressures of work were enormous and yet he was always ready to break away, to walk on Eggardon Hill or look for a sparrowhawk's nest in the Mangerton valley.

Despite his fame as a television personality, it was not widely known that he had an artificial leg – the result of a wartime accident during his time in the RAF – but despite the considerable pain it gave him it never prevented him from tramping for hours around the countryside.

At other times, dressed in a beaten-up leather flying jacket and spotted neckerchief, he loved to drive around the Dorset lanes in his flashy E-type Jaguar sports car, revealing a different side to this multi-faceted man as a style-conscious dresser, in love with the buzz of the contemporary London scene and fascinated by everything about the USA – from Western movies to Mafia mobsters and the hoboes he wrote about in *The Bootleggers* and *Hard Travellin'*.

No matter what his subject he showed himself to be a master of the English language. He loved its richness and vitality, the subtle flavours of its words, the rhythms and cadences so pleasing to the ear. His own distinctive style was often spiced with up-to-the-minute street talk. Even when describing some lyrical moment in the West Dorset countryside he could not resist lacing a sentence or two with slang if it captured to perfection the image he was trying to project.

Thus, a stoat was referred to as rippling over his shoes 'like a yellow shammy leather... an animal in crackerjack trim, like Nureyev in cream body-stocking.'

His virtuosity as a wordsmith was always an inspiration. Critics accused him of going over the top; but I loved the freshness of his metaphors and the way his copy fizzed with adjectives. Inspirational, too, was his environmental crusading. No man fought more fiercely or spoke more eloquently for the causes he believed in so deeply. 'Money speaks, beauty is voiceless,' he wrote despairingly. His detractors accused him of being trendy; yet he was fighting to preserve the graces of Britain long before words like ecology and conservation had become common currency.

In Dorset, some locals viewed him as a brash outsider; and it was true that he liked striped shirts, smart restaurants and the cut and thrust of London chatter. Yet he was hugely proud of belonging to West Dorset and it was here among the buttercup meadows and sunken lanes beneath the great limestone prow of Eggardon Hill that he was happiest, as readers of *In the Country* discovered. Published earlier that year, it had begun life as a weekly countryside column in the *Daily Mail* and became his most successful book.

When I opened Ken's book, I was thrilled to find it had a joint dedication to me and Michael Hudson, a mutual friend who was also our GP in Beaminster. The copy he sent to me also bore a hand-written inscription which I treasure: '*To Brian: pagan, pantheist, friend of the earth and sharer of the secret country – AONB 47.*'

To the very end of his life, he was the consummate journalist. I remember a photograph of him, cigarette in hand, crouched over his typewriter. All it needed was the green eyeshade to summon up the ghosts of his glory years in Fleet Street, and I suspect it revealed a fundamental truth about him, that writing was a kind of drug. It was what kept him going and continuing to write – even as he lay in bed on a misty day in May 1973, penning a letter to Betty, his wife, having already taken the overdose that would kill him, apologising for what he had done and describing the birdsong outside his window until his pen slid off the page.

Uncharacteristically, we had been talking about mortality barely a month before he died. We had been watching a pair of barn owls and the talk turned to Scotland, where I had recently found the bones of a red stag on a lonely hillside. 'That's how I would like it to be for me,' he said. 'For my body to be laid on the summit of Round Knoll. For my bones to be picked clean by the crows and just return to the earth to complete the circle.'

The funeral, like Allsop himself, was larger than life, and Powerstock had never seen anything like it. The church was filled to overflowing as reporters and media celebrities jostled for pews with villagers and family mourners. Julian Bream hushed the congregation with the bittersweet notes of his guitar. Henry Williamson stood in the pulpit, eyes blazing like an Old Testament prophet as he read out a valedictory poem in his frail old man's voice; and afterwards, outside in the churchyard beneath a tall weeping ash, the Bishop of Salisbury conducted the service of committal as friends and strangers alike stood with heads bowed in homage to the gifted, kind and tortured spirit who had burst into our lives like a comet and lit up the sky before he fell to earth.

It was good to see Henry Williamson at the funeral. Like me, the young Allsop was profoundly influenced by Williamson's nature writing to the point where he had travelled down to Devon to seek him out. The friendship flourished, even though Williamson's flirtation with fascism was anathema to him; and somehow, along with the publication of *In the Country*, it seemed to place Allsop where he truly belongs, in the pantheon of writers who have strived to repair mankind's broken covenant with the natural world.

****

The year, already blighted by Ken's death, went from bad to worse as Prime Minister Edward Heath introduced the three-day week in response to the great fuel crisis; but at least it offered me the opportunity I had been waiting for. With no end to the situation in sight, we sold up in Guildford and moved permanently to Powerstock.

When life returned to normal in March the following year there was no way I could afford to move back, but the *Sunday Times* generously allowed me to continue to work for three days every week in the office and two days at home.

Meanwhile, Harry Evans had decided to transform what he called the soft underbelly of the paper, subsuming the leisure sections – travel, gardening, motoring, and property – into a new supplement called *Scene*. Its first editor was Hunter Davies, a brilliant columnist and successful author, renowned for having written the only authorised biography of The Beatles; but it was only later, when Philip Clarke took over, that the supplement truly hit its stride. Philip had previously edited a stylish travel magazine called *Go!* before becoming a part of the *Sunday Times' Business News* section and working for him was a joy.

Besides Jean Robertson, the travel editor, my new colleagues included Graham Rose, the paper's gravel-voiced Geordie gardening correspondent, and Ian Nairn, a former RAF jet fighter pilot who had made a name for himself as an architectural correspondent with his impassioned rants against what he called the 'creeping mildew' of British post-war buildings.

Ian was a large, genial, unkempt character who fitted perfectly into the paper's menagerie of one-offs and eccentrics. When the phone rang, he had the habit of barking into it like a dog or announcing himself as 'Weasel, Stoat and Polecat', as if employed by a company of dodgy solicitors. On one such occasion the voice at the other end of the phone said: 'Do you know who this is?' Ian said he had no idea. 'This is the editor,' said the voice. 'Oh,' replied Ian, 'and do you know this is?' The editor said he did not. 'Goodbye,' said a highly relieved Ian, grinning broadly as he replaced the receiver.

Squeezed into a cheap suit, always worn with a white shirt, top button undone and tie askew, he used to scoot off around the country in his beloved Morris Minor Traveller in search of inspiration. Afterwards, back in the Gray's Inn Road, he would head for The Blue Lion and sit, pint after pint of Guinness in hand, scribbling his stories in longhand in a reporter's notebook, and nobody ever needed to change a word. Whether raging against the latest act of architectural vandalism or praising the glories of a Barnsley chop, it was always vintage Nairn until drink got the better of him and he died of cirrhosis of the liver in 1983. An inveterate nomad to the end, his last wish was granted when he asked to be buried 'somewhere under the flight path at Heathrow'.

If Philip Clarke was the captain of the ship then its first lieutenant was Richard Girling, a bearded polymath with a passion for Dartmoor who had previously edited the *Sunday Times'* letters page. Every week, he massaged my contributions into shape and once paid my writing the greatest compliment I have ever received.

'This is Brian Jackman,' he said, introducing me at a drinks party, 'he is licensed to use adjectives.'

Possibly because of our shared affinity with the West Country, we soon became the best of friends, heading off around the corner to lunch at the Kolossi Grill, a Greek Cypriot restaurant that had become the unofficial office canteen. There, having put the *Scene* pages to bed on a Friday, we would celebrate with gargantuan chunks of roast lamb and a bottle of retsina before I would sneak off early to catch the train home to Dorset.

Under the new *Scene* regime, I was given free rein to write on the burning environmental topics of the day. This was the decade when words such as ecology and conservation became common currency and Philip, with the full backing of Harry Evans, sent me to cover all kinds of assignments on everything, from whaling and Dutch elm disease to factory farming and the slaughter of our migratory songbirds on their way across the Mediterranean.

At last, I felt for the first time that I was becoming a true journalist, a fact reflected in the clothes I wore to work: faded jeans, an off-white linen jacket, the suede desert boots that had become my trademark over the years, and a variety of striped shirts that led one of my colleagues to suggest that I looked as if I had just signed on for a second-division Italian football team.

Thanks to the advice and encouragement of my fellow journalists, my new-found confidence also began to reveal itself in my writing, as revealed in a piece describing a visit to Andalusia during the Feria del Caballo, the famous Jerez Horse Fair.

> *Wine, bulls and horses. Between them they dominate*
> *this land and its people. Magical, wide open country,*

*its immense horizons drenched in the searing light of
Andalusia, and virtually treeless except where herds of
black fighting bulls roam the cork oak groves of ancestral
parklands. The rest is all grass and corn and sugar beet,
white horses running like the wind, vast marismas alive
with slowly sailing storks. And of course, the vines. Mile
after mile of hangovers reaching out in every direction.*

*Although world consumption of sherry has been declining of
late, the inhabitants of Jerez do their best to make up for it
during the Fair. Then, for two weeks, the city is gripped by horse
fever. Overnight a canvas Champs-Élysées springs up along
one of the main avenues, a rumbustious, gold-rush city devoted
to sherry, horseflesh, and flamenco. In that order.*

*Gain access to any of the roadside casetas and you are
at once plunged into a seething mass of revellers, all
firing away at each other with rapid bursts of machine-
gun Spanish. At 80p per half-bottle, the chilled dry fino
flows like water. Soon the floor is ankle-deep in empty
bottles, discarded paper cups and fading Spaniards.*

*Without warning, the air is rent by one of those ululating
cheese-grater gypsy voices. It comes from a thin brown
man with a face like Jack Palance. Cue for a song. A
rolling barrage of olés! And suddenly the whole marquee is
singing, stamping, clapping, dancing. Clap-clap-clap goes
the Jerezano rhythm. Up go the arms as the revellers twirl.
A squat, gnomish man in a sweaty shirt is pirouetting*

with a tall, elegant girl. Jack Palance is stomping and finger-snapping in his Cuban-heeled riding boots.

Everyone is singing: men in flat black hats and tight, high-waisted trousers; girls in flared denims and flouncy polka dot flamenco dresses. And horrors! A woman the width of a bodega barrel is trying to drag me into the midst of this maelstrom. Her face, pebble-dashed with acne, is split in a huge grin. No use protesting. I shuffle about in a sheepish, English sort of way but nobody cares.

Next day there are parades of magnificent horse-drawn carriages; polished phaetons and liveried coachmen from a bygone age; and the incomparable white Carthusian stallions, Elgin marbles come to life, swollen crested necks bedecked with bright tassels, dancing to a paso doble.

During my stay a full programme of excursions had been arranged by the local tourist office; but somehow there always seemed to be too many bodegas, too many nights when I stayed too long at the Fair. In the end I got no further than the Parador at Arcos de la Frontera, balanced on the brink of a dizzy yellow cliff where tawny hawks swung in the up-draughts and the sound of nightingales floated up from the river below. One day I must go back and see the bits I missed.

By now, Harry was in his fifties and had just discovered the joys and tribulations of skiing. I had been skiing regularly ever since my days with Poly Travel and could now describe myself as a reasonably accomplished red-run cruiser. The result was a summons to the editor's office.

Harry had a problem, he told me. He had been looking everywhere for a book that would teach him how to be a better skier but had been unable to find anything suitable. 'They're all written for experts,' he complained. 'There's nothing suitable for beginners like me.' So, being Harry, he had decided that the *Sunday Times* should produce one ourselves. 'How would you like to work on a ski book for a couple of weeks?' he asked.

It was a command, of course, and not a question, but I could not have been happier. The two weeks extended for 18 months – including long spells at Wengen in the Bernese Oberland – and I became a co-editor together with Harry and Mark Ottaway, a talented refugee from the News Desk who had joined the travel pages.

The result was *We Learned to Ski*. First published in 1974, it became an international bestseller whose royalties kept me in funds for several years; but its real rewards were the long days I spent on the slopes with Alasdair Ross, the senior trainer for the British Association of Ski Instructors.

Ali Ross was a crofter's son, a wiry Scot with gunslinger's shanks. 'The man with the talking legs,' I called him, since you only needed to see him demonstrating the art of the parallel turn to know exactly what to do. It came as no surprise to discover he was the first Briton ever to be employed by the Swiss Ski School in Wengen, and our time together in the shadow of the Eiger not only forged a friendship which has lasted to this day but also improved my skiing beyond all recognition.

Suddenly, one day with Ali at Wengen in the shadow of the Eiger, everything clicked, and I found myself carving turn after effortless turn through an overnight dusting of diamond-bright powder snow. It was as if I was skiing on automatic pilot, one turn leading instinctively into the next, to a rhythm as precise as a pendulum, and no thought beyond the high-octane euphoria of that headlong rush down the fall line.

Fellow fanatics will know the feeling. It happens when the snow is flattering and forgiving, when edges bite, when confidence is absolute and every swooping turn induces that stomach-lifting sensation – not of skiing down the mountain but of flying, held fast to the snow by nothing but the whisper of gravity under your skis. That was the gift that Ali gave me.

******

In between my trips to Wengen I continued to write for the travel pages, seeking out wilderness wherever it occurred, including a memorable trek in Norway with a wartime hero.

Claus Helberg was a living legend, one of the nine Heroes of Telemark, the resistance team that blew up the Nazi's heavy water plant at Rjukan in 1943. When I met him, he had become the inspector of the Norwegian Mountain Touring Association, and together we were going to climb Høgronden, a hulking 7,000-foot (2,114-metre) brute of a mountain in the Rondane Mountains National Park.

A thin, whipcord man with barbed-wire eyebrows and a puckish, slightly mocking face, Helberg spoke slowly, recalling his incredible exploits when he and eight companions succeeded in blowing to smithereens all Nazi hopes of building an atomic bomb.

As for Høgronden, it was how you might imagine Odin's graveyard, a crazy stairway of what looked like shattered tombstones disappearing into the clouds above us. Having finally reached the summit, the descent was even more arduous, pussyfooting down dizzy ridges that fell sheer on both sides into a misty void. We walked to the constant sound of rushing water, marvelling at the beauty of the high mountain tarns – some a magical jade green and others still opaque with last winter's ice. Even in midsummer the Rondane mountains were piebald with snow, and we tramped across snowdrifts imprinted with reindeer tracks in this untamed corner of subarctic Europe where wolverine, gyrfalcons, and fearsomely shaggy musk ox live, but are almost never seen.

At the touring hut at Dørålseter a hot dinner awaited in a snug pine room with a pot-bellied stove. To get there had taken us nine hours of non-stop walking to cover the 16 up-and-down miles from the turf-topped farmstead at Bjørnhollia where we had spent the previous night. Yet in all that time, while I was wolfing sandwiches from my rucksack, Helberg took nothing but a few gulps of ice-cold water scooped from a mountain stream.

After supper I was so exhausted that I fell asleep in front of the stove and awoke to find him staring at me. 'You know,' he said with a strange, faraway look in his eyes, 'you look so incredibly English.' I can only imagine he was thinking back to the time when he and his British commando counterparts took on the might of the German armed forces.

****

Unlike Norway's Rondane mountains, our summers in Powerstock were sheer bliss. Even in winter we usually managed to avoid the worst weather encountered upcountry. Until 1978 – the year of the blizzard that buried Dorset.

It began innocently enough; just an overnight dusting of snow, although preceding frosts had been the hardest for over a decade. The following night we received another light snowfall, enabling the village children to turn out in force next morning with toboggans.

But the day which had dawned bright and clear changed as the weekend approached. The sky turned leaden, the wind swung round to the east and at lunchtime on Saturday it began to snow again – not soft, fat Yuletide flakes but a pitiless blast of frost-sharpened powder which settled fast. In the evening, friends were due from Beaminster, five miles away, but could not make it because the roads were blocked.

On Sunday I awoke to a scene of pure Antarctica. Five feet of snow lay piled against the door. Outside, it was impossible to walk even a dozen steps without floundering waist-deep, so I took down my skis from the attic and set out to explore.

The high winds had flung great drifts against walls and hedgerows. On hills and bank tops huge frozen cornices hung like Atlantic breakers in mid-curl. The sunken lanes had been filled in so deeply with snow that I could cross from hedge to hedge with the road 15 feet beneath, over cars buried where they had been abandoned with only their radio aerials visible.

At one spot on the downs above us the snow was so deep it was even possible to sit on top of the telegraph poles. In beleaguered Bridport, the townsfolk made snowmen in the middle of the main street. Snow bergs floated in West Bay harbour, where pounding seas had punched a 60-yard hole in the promenade, and over everything lay the unaccustomed silence of a world without traffic.

In the afternoon, a force-10 storm was blowing off Portland Bill and driving still more snow across an Ice Age Dorset. That night foxes and roe deer ran hungry through the village gardens; their prints were clear to see next day. Small birds perished where they hid in hedgerows. Robins and blackbirds pecked ravenously at garden scraps, and Aunt Isobel, then the oldest resident in the village, declared she had seen nothing like it in all her 90 years.

Television and radio bulletins began to sketch in the full effects of what an emergency edition of the local paper described as 'The Great White Straitjacket' in which the entire West Country was paralysed: schools closed; roads stopped up by mammoth drifts; Yeovil, Dorchester and Barnstaple cut off; Dartmoor and Exmoor rendered impassable.

Phone calls to friends filled in local gaps. Forage was dropped for animals marooned on Eggardon Hill whose Iron Age earthworks held 20 feet of snow. Dead sheep were being dug out and fed to pigs, and thousands of gallons of milk had to be poured down the drain. In short, it spelt heartbreak and near-disaster for many Dorset farmers.

Like most villagers, we survived comfortably. Hearing the weather forecast in London, I had prudently left early and arrived home in time to be snowed in. There was no lack of food or fuel; bread was home-baked, and milk was being given away. We dug out an elderly lady whose cottage was half-buried, and I ran a Samaritan errand on skis, taking pills to a housebound arthritic sufferer in the next valley.

By Wednesday, the thaw had set in. Meltwater was pouring off the hills and tractors were working round the clock as farmers cleared the lanes with scrapers in a desperate battle to get their milk to market.

Now flooding was the fear, for the sodden ground could hold no more. Swollen streams roared in the surrounding combes and heavy rain was forecast, reminding people of an earlier occasion when, allegedly, a grand piano was seen sailing down the valley with the survivors of a wrecked hen coop clucking on its superstructure.

Fortunately, the heavy rain missed Dorset, although at Kingsbridge in Devon and out on the Somerset Levels around Taunton, houses were flooded to a depth of several feet as rivers burst their banks and drowned the fields for miles around.

By the following week, the temperature had climbed dizzily into the fifties. Celandines bloomed and skylarks sang over Eggardon, as if celebrating nature's astounding resilience. Spring, a ludicrous proposition only days before, was on its way. But heaped under every westward-facing hedgerow and running like a white scar below the western lip of the downs, relic drifts still lay 10 feet deep in places, and the last snow did not melt until well into March.

CHAPTER SIXTEEN

TWO years after my first visit to Africa I was back again in the Mara, staying at a bush camp run by Jock Anderson, the genial owner of a company called East African Wildlife Safaris. One of his guides was a young Englishman who had hitchhiked around Africa in search of a job and pitched up here beside the Mara River. His name was Jonathan Scott – now renowned all over the world as one of Africa's finest wildlife photographers.

Jonathan it was who became my guide and we immediately struck up a friendship that would last a lifetime. He wanted to show me a pride of lions he had been following. The core of their territory was Musiara Marsh in the north of the reserve near Governor's Camp, an area that provided everything lions need: shade and water, plentiful hiding places where they could raise their cubs, and an abundance of food all year round.

During the dry season, the migrating wildebeest and zebra would come to drink at the Marsh every day and the lions would lie up in the reeds and ambush them. The Marsh Lions, Jonathan called them, and when we decided to write a true story of their triumphs and travails, that became its title. Neither of us knew it then, but three decades later the Marsh pride would become the world's most famous lions as the feline superstars of the BBC's *Big Cat Diary* television series.

Those days spent in their company were among the happiest of my life, and what a privilege it was to enter their world and come to know them as individuals, each one as recognisable to us as an old friend, in the same way a shepherd knows his sheep.

At night I would awake to hear them roaring, and the magic never failed. '*Hii nchi ya nani?*' is their message when translated into Swahili. 'Whose land is this?' Then, as their tumultuous challenge dies away, they answer with a rhythmic coda of rasping grunts that make the air vibrate; *yangu, yangu, yangu*, mine, mine, mine!

Sometimes, observing Scar, Brando and Mkubwa, as we called the three Marsh pride males, I would try to imagine what it must feel like to be a lion. Like me, they would have smelt the grass and heard the sad cries of wood doves in the noontide *luggas* – the bush-choked seasonal watercourses in which they took their rest. Did we not feel the same sense of pleasure when the sun warmed us on a cold morning? Thirst, hunger, aggression, fear; there were many sensations we must have shared, but what else went on behind those implacable eyes would forever remain a mystery.

So habituated did the Marsh Lions become to our presence that sometimes, far out on the treeless plains, the pride males would seek out Jonathan's vehicle and slump in its shade, panting harshly in the blistering heat as they lay within touching distance for hours on end; but only once did we ever experience a potentially risky moment.

It happened back in camp one afternoon when I had joined Jonathan for tea in his tent. I had been there no more than a few minutes than one of the camp staff came rushing up in great agitation. '*Bwana*,' he said to Jonathan, 'we have a *simba* in camp!'

Without hesitation Jonathan leapt to his feet, grabbed a canvas-backed seat, and stepped outside, leaving me with no option but to follow him.

Sure enough, there was the lion, a big, shaggy male, standing no more than a few metres away. For a moment there was a stand-off, with the two of us holding our chairs in front of us, confronting the lion we recognised instantly as Brando, one of the three territorial pride males. Then, with a gruff 'whoof' expelled through his half-closed jaws, he turned and trotted away through the riverine forest. As he did so, we noticed a noise above our heads, and there was our cook, halfway up a tree where he had taken refuge when the lion arrived.

Afterwards, when my pulse had returned to normal, I started thinking about the macho posturing of trophy hunters, proudly posing for a picture beside the carcass of the lion they have just gunned down, with their professional hunter in attendance as additional insurance in case anything should go wrong. If you fancy a real adrenaline rush, I thought, why not put aside your gun and try confronting a lion at close range with nothing but a chair to defend yourself as we did?

Looking back now I can see that the life of the Marsh Pride in those glory days was a golden age for the big cats and the boundless savannahs of their savage kingdom. To a casual eye it was a serene and shining landscape, as peaceful as an English park. There was no malice in it, no hint of suffering or hostility. Orioles called with clear voices from the dappled shade of forest figs. Hippos chuckled in the river, and boubou shrikes chimed their monotonous xylophonic responses from the heat-drugged thickets. The sounds of summer lulled the senses; but the world of the plains animals was a constant paradox. Nothing was ever what it seemed. Tranquillity was an illusion behind which stalked old familiar spectres: hunger, thirst, disease. Those golden vistas, outwardly so innocent and benign, were

Above left In the garden at 34 Briarwood.
Above centre Wearing my father's Home Guard forage cap.
Above right Taken around the time I was about to be evacuated.

Above With my mother and father and Spike, their terrier.

Above left With cousin Peter and our homemade bows and arrows.
Above right Football mad – wearing my father's Wimbledon FC socks.

Above On Polzeath beach with my father and brothers.

Above left Able Seaman Jackman, RN, taken at home on leave in 1953.
Above right Manning the Bofors gun onboard HMS *Welcome*, 1954.

Above HMS *Welcome*, the minesweeper that was my home for 18 months.

Above With Geoff Lanegan (left), friends since I was four years old.

Above left In full voice at the Skiffle Cellar in Greek Street, Soho.
Above right The Eden Street Skiffle Group (me on the right).

Above On Porthmeor beach, St Ives, in my early twenties.

Above The West Bay Flowers (me front row, second left, and Ian Stewart
of the Rolling Stones, far right).

Above left Imogen, my daughter, in her highchair.

Above right Imogen aged five, growing up in the countryside.

Above Teaching Imogen how to master the snowplough turn.

Above Skiing in fresh powder snow at Wengen, in the Swiss Alps.

Above The *Sunday Times* team behind *We Learned to Ski*
(Harold Evans front row on left).

Above 'The most contented man I ever met.' George Adamson
and his pipe at Kora. (Photo © Tony Fitzjohn)

Above George Adamson and two of his orphaned lions at Kora,
in northern Kenya. (Photo © Tony Fitzjohn)

Above Who could fail not to be obsessed with lions?

Above left With Tony Fitzjohn, George Adamson's indispensable
second-in-command at Kora.

Above right With Virginia McKenna, who played Joy Adamson in
the film version of *Born Free*.

Left With Jonathan Scott, who introduced me to the Marsh Lions in 1974.

Above Scar in his prime; one of the Marsh Pride's three resident males in 1974.

Above Jackson ole Looseyia, the distinguished Maasai safari guide who became a co-presenter on the BBC's *Big Cat Diary*.

Above The day I met Abu, the elephant on whose broad back I rode in Botswana.

Above Abu's Camp in the Okavango was also the home of
Valentina, a tame fishing owl.

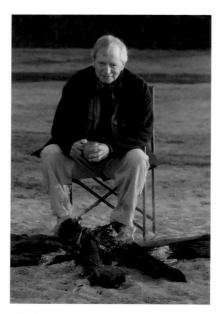

Above Early morning tea, Luangwa Valley, Zambia.

Above Exploring South Luangwa with Robin Pope (centre).

Above left Receiving the British Guild of Travel Writer's Travel Writer
of the Year award.

Above right The spot beneath the Brèche, where I was nearly killed
by a falling rock.

Above Crossing the Pyrenees on my 50th birthday.

Above With Iain Douglas-Hamilton at his Save the Elephants HQ in Samburu, Kenya.

Above A pet genet encountered while reporting on the ivory wars in Tsavo.

Above Making friends with an orphaned cheetah at Okonjima, home of the AfriCat Foundation in Namibia.

THE SUNDAY TIMES magazine

WILD THING!

Above My parting gift on leaving the *Sunday Times*:
a dummy cover of the magazine.

Above Breakfast time with one of the residents at Giraffe Manor in Nairobi.

Left Waiting for take-off on an *Out of Africa* biplane joyride at Samburu game reserve.

Left Lion tracking in Kenya's Chyulu Hills National Park.

Left The author in Africa.

Left At John Stevens' camp in Mana Pools National Park, 2018.

Above 'The most hospitable people on Earth' – Maasai camp staff in the Mara.

Above left Annabelle – our wedding in Aldeburgh in 1993.

Above right Home sweet home in the Kalahari.

Above On safari together in elephant country: Old Mondoro in
Lower Zambezi National Park.

Left On safari in style; seeing the Mara by helicopter.

Left Indian Ocean idyll: the sandbanks of Benguerra off the Mozambique coast.

Above Meeting the meerkats at Jack's Camp in the Makgadikgadi.

Above With Christopher Swann – aka Swanny the Whale-Whisperer.

Above left Annabelle – the Girl with the North Sea Eyes.
Above right Looking for blue whales in the Sea of Cortez.

Above Waiting for the 'Ice Bears' of Arctic Yukon.

Above Grizzly mother and cub – the 'Ice Bears' of Yukon's Fishing Branch River.

Above Eggardon Hill – where the real West Country begins.

Above 'If ever a house was meant to be ours, Spick Hatch was the one.'

Above left The stone lion carved by our friend Eva Harvey.
Above right The only black rhino in Dorset – made of marine plywood and set
up in the orchard.

Above left Away to the meadow to cut the hay.

Above Summer in the garden and fresh strawberries for lunch.

Left Luca and Jude, my grandchildren in the orchard.

Above Happy ever after.

full of sudden, violent images. The pristine plains were a charnel house of skulls and bones, half-eaten zebras, bloated vultures. Hidden in the tall grass, slovenly hyenas raised gory muzzles from a shipwreck of ribs, and hungry lions tore at their kills with paws encased in gloves of blood.

All this I discovered and none of it dissuaded me. Rather, it drew me even deeper into the timeless world of the African plains. There would be other lions along the way: the Kalahari males with their big black manes, the buffalo-killers of Duba Plains in Botswana, and the lion that prowled around me one night while fly camping beside the Ngare Ndare sand river in northern Kenya. But none would I ever know so well as the Marsh Lions of the Masai Mara where my life with lions began.

****

The most extraordinary lion behaviour I ever witnessed took place at Kora, where George Adamson of *Born Free* fame lived in the wilds of northern Kenya.

It happened in January 1980, the day after Joy Adamson's funeral in Nairobi. Only two months earlier I had been interviewing her at her camp in the Shaba game reserve. Now the world-famous author of *Born Free* – the bestselling story of an orphaned lion cub – was dead, murdered by one of her former camp staff.

When the news reached the *Sunday Times*, I was sent to Nairobi to cover the story and it was there I met the grand old Lion Man of Kenya for the first time. By then the couple had long since separated. George said he much preferred the company of his lions to that of his wife and invited me to meet them.

Having filed my story, I flew back to Kora with him, where the first thing we did was to jump into his decrepit old Land Rover and set off into the bush.

We stopped on the banks of the Tana River, and George got out. 'Arusha,' he shouted, in the way you might call for your dog. 'Come on, old girl.' And at the sound of his voice, she emerged from a thorn thicket, a full-grown lioness with blood on her muzzle from the waterbuck she had just killed.

What happened next is engraved forever on my mind. From where I sat in the front of the vehicle, I watched spellbound as the lioness ran at him, then rose on her hind legs and draped her huge forepaws over the old man's shoulders, grunting with pleasure as he hugged her tawny body and made little moaning lion noises of his own in reply.

The extraordinary saga of *Born Free* brought international acclaim for Joy but led George, her retired game-warden husband, to Kora, where he would devote the rest of his life to the high-risk business of returning lions to the wild.

'I chose Kora because it was the only place where I was allowed to bring my lions,' George told me. 'It was a sort of no man's land that nobody wanted.' He rented it from the local council – £750 a year for 500 miles of unforgiving wilderness straddling the Equator – and built a home he called *Kampi ya Simba*: Lion Camp.

Here he lived in a wire compound with his raggle-taggle pride of rescued lions roaming free on the other side. Among them was Boy, who had starred with Virginia McKenna in the *Born Free* movie, and Christian, a fifth-generation zoo lion who had come to Kora via Harrods and a King's Road furniture shop.

Among the human residents that shared George's extraordinary existence were his brother Terence, Hamisi his devoted cook, and Tony Fitzjohn, a wild young Englishman with shoulder-length hair and sawn-off shorts who had hitchhiked to Kenya to work with animals.

Like the lions, Fitzjohn was an orphan. He was also tough and capable and could turn his hand to anything, from stripping down a Land Rover to fixing the two-way radio. Best of all, when working with the big cats, he turned out to be a natural.

Life at Kora was simple but never dull, as I discovered on subsequent visits. Even going to the *choo* (lavatory) was an adventure as the camp latrine consisted of an upturned elephant's jawbone strategically balanced on two planks.

Not all the wildlife lived beyond the wire. Over the years, Adamson shared his camp with a multitude of creatures. Ground squirrels begged for peanuts and hopped among the dinner plates, looking for leftovers. Crikey and Croaky, a pair of fan-tailed ravens that bred on Kora's crags hopped in for tea. Bourne and Hollingsworth, a couple of hooded vultures, sat on the fence, and a monitor lizard the length of my arm and known inexplicably as Guildford slept in the dining room thatch.

They were happy days, but they could not last. Fast-forward to August 1989. By now, George was 84 and had just learned that Kora was to be made a national park when he was shot dead by Somali bandits. The world mourned his passing and the eulogies poured in. Africa had lost a warrior for conservation and I had lost a friend.

******

Lions were not the only animals that would have a profound influence on my life. When I was still new to Africa, I went into Zambia's Kafue National Park on a walking safari with a veteran guide called Cecil Evans. He was as tough and bush wise as they come and was known to his friends as *Nyama Yangu* (Swahili for 'My Meat'), a name acquired through his habit of chasing lions off their kill and helping himself to a juicy zebra steak.

The bush was dense in places and I was relieved to see that he carried a rifle. We had not gone far when, without warning, an extremely grumpy bull elephant exploded from the trees and came straight for us, head held high and screaming like an express train.

I still remember Evans' words. 'Stay where you are and don't run,' he commanded, a singularly useless piece of advice since my legs had turned to jelly.

He stepped forward, slapping the butt of his gun and shouting obscenities at the enraged tusker, which skidded to a halt just a few metres away, shaking its huge, ragged ears as it towered over us.

There followed a nail-biting stand-off which ended only when Evans took off his bush hat and hurled it at the elephant, screaming 'Bugger off!' at the top of his voice, at which the big bull spun around and lumbered off, ripping up a sapling as it did so and smashing it on the ground as if to say, 'That's what I'd like to do to you.'

Prior to that encounter I had been somewhat shy by nature, always apprehensive when meeting people who were older than myself or those whom I considered to be my superiors. As a journalist this had been a particularly awkward problem. Now it had vanished overnight. After all, what could anyone say that could be more terrifying than standing up to an angry elephant?

To this day I have always had the greatest respect for elephants, but it was not until I visited Abu's Camp in Botswana's Okavango Delta that I truly began to understand them. There is a long-held belief that African elephants, unlike their Asian cousins, are treacherous, unpredictable, and impossible to train. But Randall Jay Moore, a cigar-smoking American biologist, Vietnam War protester and animal trainer, turned conventional wisdom on its head by offering elephant-riding safaris in the Okavango when he arrived there in 1990.

'Elephants are a lot smarter than a lot of people I've met,' he told me. 'They never lie or let you down. Their social structure is so like ours in so many ways, and all the best qualities we have as humans I see in my elephants every day.'

Abu, Benny, and Cathy, his three riding elephants, were re-introduced to Africa from zoos and circuses in America, where they had been originally sent as orphans. Together they formed the nucleus of Abu's herd, which expanded in Botswana with the arrival of seven baby elephants – survivors of a cull in South Africa's Kruger National Park.

Abu himself was probably the most famous elephant in the world, having starred in several films including *White Hunter, Black Heart*, in which he appeared alongside Clint Eastwood. He was born in the wild in 1960, but then captured and transported to the USA where he grew up in a Texas safari park. That was where Randall found him, chained in a barn, and sleeping in his own dung on a bare concrete floor.

On an impulse, Randall offered to buy Abu for $10,000. 'It was the best deal I ever made,' he said. It was also the beginning of an extraordinary partnership that would last until Abu died of a heart attack in 2002 after a fight with a wild elephant.

When I met Abu, he was in his prime, and for five never-to-be-forgotten days I rode with him and his herd, rocking and swaying through the reeds, feeling his huge spine flexing beneath me as we splashed across the Delta's floodplains on a slow march to paradise.

Sometimes, instead of riding I walked with Randall at my side, and it was then, as we followed in Abu's giant footsteps through a backlit haze of golden grass heads amid a forest of pillared legs and flapping ears, that I sensed what it might feel like to be an elephant, a member of a close-knit family bound by kinship ties as complex as our own. Looking up into Abu's benign brown eyes with their long dark lashes, I felt humbled by their tolerance, and to walk with them was to come tantalisingly close to bridging the gulf that separates us from the rest of the world.

CHAPTER SEVENTEEN

IN 1981 when Rupert Murdoch's News International bought the *Sunday Times* from the Thompson Corporation, everyone knew the paper would never be the same again. When Harry Evans became editor of *The Times,* Frank Giles, his deputy, took over the helm and for a while life in Gray's Inn Road carried on much as before.

One of my travel assignments that year was a press trip to Zambia, where I met Norman Carr, the legendary grand old man of the Luangwa Valley who reinvented the old-fashioned foot safari. At that time, the South Luangwa National Park was an unknown wilderness with fewer than a handful of bush camps; but over the next 35 years it would become one of Africa's most sought-after safari destinations, part of a billion-dollar industry whose revenues would be indispensable in underwriting the survival of the world's wildlife and last wild places.

Thanks largely to the piece I wrote about my introduction to bush-bashing with Norman in the Luangwa, I was thrilled to be awarded the British Guild of Travel Writers' prestigious Travel Writer of the Year award in 1982. To my great surprise I also won the BBC's award for the best wildlife film commentary of 1982. This was for *Osprey,* an hour-long documentary shot by Hugh Miles, a hugely talented film-maker who worked for the RSPB and later went on to win a whole string of awards for the BBC's Natural History Unit in Bristol with films such as *Kingdom of the Ice Bear.*

Hugh had been inspired by the television films Eric Ashby had made in the 1960s on the wildlife of the New Forest and had learned how to gain the trust of the animals he was filming by wearing the same clothes day after day and following the same routine – a technique he had copied after reading J.A. Baker's book, *The Peregrine*. Whether filming otters in Shetland or pumas in Patagonia, it enabled him to produce close-up portraits of his subjects which previous film-makers had never managed to capture. He also had a keen eye for a story and saw in me a kindred spirit, resulting in a friendship that has continued to flourish ever since.

One of my most memorable assignments that year was a trip to Ardnamurchan, one of the most remote and inhospitable places in Britain, to meet a writer who had withdrawn from the world like a wounded beast to chronicle the life of a golden eagle.

Mike Tomkies was a born loner. At school in Sussex during the 1930s his best subject was divinity, but he soon turned away from orthodox religion, believing that Christianity demeans nature by putting man above the animals. Instead, he became fascinated by butterflies and left school with a burning ambition to become a gamekeeper. The job did not last and in 1946 he joined the Coldstream Guards, which led to sentry duty at Buckingham Palace and active service in Palestine. Then one day he bought Tolstoy's *War and Peace*. He read it four times and bought himself out, determined to become a writer.

His first reward was a 35-shillings-a-week job with the *Chichester Observer*, producing a column called 'Pulpit and Pew'. Then, in 1955, came the *Daily Mail* and a rising reputation as a crime reporter, during which time he met the notorious gangsters Jack Spot and the Kray twins. Then came a lucky break. An exclusive interview with the film star Ava Gardner enabled him to break into the glittering world of celebrity journalism, and thus began a decade of fast cars and endless parties, dates with the world's most beautiful women, jetting between Rome, St Tropez and Hollywood to meet Errol Flynn, John Wayne and Marilyn Monroe.

It all ended at the age of 38. Disillusioned with showbiz and hurt by a couple of broken romances, he impulsively gave away his London flat and flew to Canada, where he worked as a logger and salmon-boat deckhand before building a cabin and living like Thoreau in the backwoods of British Columbia.

There he remained until one day he found a tattered copy of Gavin Maxwell's *Ring of Bright Water*. Overwhelmed by nostalgia he returned home and eventually found what he was looking for, a deserted croft on the wrong side of a loch deep in the desolate tangle of wild hills and glens west of Fort William. Its last regular tenant had left in 1912. There was no road, no electricity, gas, TV, or telephone. His only luxury was water piped in from a burn; his only companion a three-legged Alsatian called Moobli. The living room was a flotsam of antlers, skulls, seashells, and eagle feathers. On the desk, a tilley lamp and a beaten-up typewriter; and here, surrounded by his favourite authors – Tolstoy, Nietzsche, Henry Williamson – he struggled to make a living as a writer, forsaking human contact in order to pursue golden eagles.

Now his book was complete, the culmination of a nine-year obsession with Britain's most iconic birds of prey, hence my visit. He needed publicity and had cautiously agreed to take me to find his birds, telling me that in all that time I was only his fourth visitor.

At first the hills seemed lifeless except for the deer keeping watch on the skyline. Ears cocked in V-signs of derision, they observed us until we reached a corrie, an immense amphitheatre among the high tops, and then streamed away out of sight.

The day was sultry and overcast, the air alive with biting flies. But on the summit, coolness breathed, and I could hear golden plovers not far off. Their haunting cries hung in the wind, sad as a piper's lament.

Below us lay a glen of aching loneliness, a burn winding silver at its bottom. We zigzagged down to scoop sweet water in cupped hands as it spilled through the rocks, then climbed another thousand feet towards a sentinel rowan standing guard beside a crag.

Across the glen the summits swung away into the high trailing mist, their sullen faces as grey as sleet. And suddenly she was there: the veteran female whom Mike Tomkies called Atalanta, after the Greek princess of the Calydonian boar hunt. A huge, dark shape, claws bunched beneath her, sailing on her seven-foot wingspan towards the opposite hillside.

Almost at once we heard a shrill cry and looked up to see Atalanta's eaglet, now fully fledged, lofting out from the crags above us. Tomkies breathed a sigh of relief. Here was living proof that another young eagle had been safely raised.

Afterwards we saw Atalanta's eyrie, empty now, a great stick pile on a ledge with the mummified leg of a red deer fawn dangling in the wind.

Back at the croft, Tomkies poured me a tumbler of whisky, said we had covered 12 miles, climbed a total of 8,000 feet and told me I had done well on the hill. I was too knackered to reply; but fatigue took second place to a feeling of exultation. For I had been to the land of the eagles, to the realm of the high corries and hanging clouds, among the great sad hills and haunted glens, and experienced, albeit fleetingly, the joys and loneliness of this indomitable man.

****

In 1983, following the fiasco over the Hitler Diaries, Frank Giles was replaced as editor of the *Sunday Times* by Andrew Neil. The diaries, allegedly purporting to have been written in Hitler's own hand, turned out to be a fake and Giles' distinguished career was in ruins.

There could not have been a greater difference between Giles, an urbane and mild-mannered academic, and his successor. Andrew Neil was an ambitious political bruiser, built like a rugby prop forward and possessed of an intellect sharpened at Glasgow University where he edited the student newspaper. With Murdoch's backing he moved the paper's political opinions farther to the right than they had ever been under Harry Evans.

One of the few things both men had in common was their love of skiing, and one of Neil's first endeavours at the *Sunday Times* was to produce a series of *Ski Perfect* videos with Ali Ross, as if anything Harry could do, he could do better. I asked Ali what he thought of Neil's technique on the slopes. His raised eyebrows said it all. 'He skis like a telephone box,' he said.

These were turbulent times for all of us, and I had the distinct impression that conservation and the environment were not at the top of Neil's agenda. 'If he can't f*** it or plug it into the mains he doesn't want to know,' was one of the comments going around the office. Somehow it reached his ears, and to his credit he had the words framed and hung in his office, although he never found out which of us had coined the remark.

In 1984 *The Marsh Lions* was published. Thanks to widespread publicity, during which I was invited to take part in BBC Radio's *Pick of the Week*, it became a bestseller, acclaimed as an African wildlife classic. Its success would launch Jonathan Scott's career, from award-winning photographer to popular presenter of the BBC's long-running *Big Cat Diary* TV series and author of a succession of coffee-table books on the big cats and other denizens of the Masai Mara. As for me, when Philip Clarke became editor of the *Sunday Times Magazine,* I accompanied him and became a feature writer for what was then considered to represent the best of British journalism – something I never considered in my wildest dreams when I joined the paper.

Most of my stories on the magazine still revolved around conservation and travel and I loved seeing them accompanied by stunning colour photography. In 1985 I also completed another book. *The Countryside in Winter* was the result of a series of journeys I had made around Britain during the previous couple of years and owed much of its success to the evocative watercolour illustrations of Bruce Pearson, a renowned wildlife artist who used to tramp around the countryside on location with all his paints and other belongings in a tea chest strapped to his back.

The book was conceived as a celebration of winter, beginning with the richness and decay of autumn when all wildlife prepares for the lean months ahead and ending in March when the land emerges shriven and renewed to greet the returning spring. Anyone can love Britain in the summer, I felt, but winter is a connoisseur's season, its colours muted, miraculous and austere. When the leaves are down it is easier to appreciate the tracery of trees and the stark simplicity of bare horizons. The fields are open to the sky. The lanes are full of foxy smells. The summer visitors have gone, and the elemental countryside comes into its own.

The result was an irregular diary, recording observations around my home in Dorset and those made on forays all over Britain to see some of the spectacular species which add so much drama to the land in winter.

One of the most enjoyable trips was made the previous year and involved looking for red kites with Roger Lovegrove in the hills of mid-Wales. Roger was a former physical education teacher who worked for the Royal Society for the Protection of Birds. For more than two decades he had been one of their most steadfast guardians, watching over the welfare of the birds of Wales from the RSPB regional office at Newtown in Powys. A tall, lean man, his face furrowed by long days out of doors, he bubbled with energy and eloquence in equal measure, and his knowledge of Wales and its birds was unsurpassed.

Together we followed the River Ystwyth into one of the loveliest valleys in mid-Wales. We passed Hafod church and came at last to a high lane among lonely hills with thick woods of oak and larch reaching towards us, and the Ystwyth writhing in silver coils through the meadows below.

It was mid-January, and squalls of hail swept the hills, followed by a strange, granular snow that dusted the summits and settled like hoar frost in the lane. We parked in a lay-by looking down into a vertiginous valley and waited for the red kites which Lovegrove knew would soon come drifting in to roost among the oaks beneath us.

The return of the red kite is a remarkable success story for British conservation and the RSPB. It was not always a rare bird. In Elizabethan times red kites were regular scavengers in the streets of London and remained common until the late 18th century. But then followed the age of intensive game preservation in which all predators were regarded as vermin, and the red kite never stood a chance. By 1870 it had gone from England. Thirty years later the last Scottish red kite had been wiped out, leaving the hills of central Wales as the bird's last refuge. Here at the turn of the century a handful of pairs survived among the remote and un-keepered valleys and clung on long enough for more enlightened views to prevail.

Since then, the red kite has clawed its way back from the brink of extinction, but even at the time of my visit in the 1980s its presence was the motivating spark which gave the wild Welsh hills their tension. In kite country there is always a tingling sense of anticipation, and I scoured the hilltops, yearning for a glimpse of that rakish silhouette, the long wings bent against the pluck of wind, and a fanned form tail – the kite's true trademark – deep-etched against the winter sky.

Now, singly and in pairs, the first birds began to arrive, sailing and circling over the head of the valley. By day kites hunt alone or in pairs, scavenging for dead sheep or rabbits, sometimes travelling up to 15 miles but always returning to their communal winter roost among the sheltering oaks.

At one point I had six red kites in view. Later I counted nine spiralling together. They flew in the teeth of the wind, heedless of the slanting snow which reduced the more distant birds to wraiths. Some passed within 50 feet of where we sat, and one came so close I could see every detail of its plumage, as if in a measured drawing. Its body and wing coverts were brown and tawny like November oaks. The red tail drew its colour from the dead bracken, and the head and wing patches were as one with the hills under their dusting of snow.

And still they came, rocking and swaying on crooked wings, riding in on the blizzard as dusk began to fall around us. We counted at least 30: one quarter of all the red kites of Wales that year. Even Roger Lovegrove was thrilled. 'In 20 years of birdwatching in Wales,' he said, 'that is the most I have seen in a single day.'

******

By now I had reached what I thought was the ripe old age of 50 and was wondering how to mark this milestone when I received a call from Robin Neillands, a fellow travel writer and ex Royal Marine who was the same age as me and had devised a series of adventures to celebrate the occasion. Among them, he said, was a three-day high-altitude hike over the Pyrenees from Spain into France, and would I like to join him?

We set off from Torla, the mountain village that stands at the entrance to the Ordesa and Monte Perdido National Park. Ordesa is Spain's answer to the Grand Canyon and a strong contender for the most beautiful park in Europe. Its lower depths are an earthly paradise of fathomless beechwoods filled with the sound of the Rio Arazas as it leaps and crashes down the valley on its way to the scorching plains of Aragon. Its upper limits are the sky-high rimrocks of the canyon walls, weathered into fantastic shapes, with huge prows and pinnacles and brooding citadels of tawny limestone that turn to gold in the evening light.

The first few kilometres were easy, but soon the path began to rise more steeply until at last it emerged above the treeline in a different world of high mountain pastures where gentians bloomed and the air tasted sharper. Here we camped (illegally, we later discovered) in the great amphitheatre of the Circo de Soaso, whose headwalls close in around this classic U-shaped glacial valley. Next morning there was frost on the tents, but long before mid-morning we were walking in shirtsleeves again.

For centuries, the Pyrenees have acted as a natural barrier, cutting off Spain from the rest of Europe. The Moors called them El Hadjiz – the barricade – the great wall between the dusty brown African landscapes of Iberia and the green fields of France, 435 kilometres of jagged peaks and crests running from the Bay of Biscay to the Mediterranean.

The Romans used the few high passes as imperial trade routes, and medieval pilgrims following the road to Santiago de Compostela toiled over the Col de Somport on their way to the shrine of St James the Moor-slayer; but for the most part the Pyrenees remained aloof from the mainstream of history. Only occasionally, as in AD778 when the Basques butchered Charlemagne's rearguard in the Col de Roncesvalles, did the sounds of war disturb the mountains' ancient silence. And silent they remained well into the 20th century, lonely and untrodden except by shepherds and hunters, a refuge for bandits, a stronghold for smugglers and a favourite wartime escape route used by the Resistance for helping RAF pilots to flee Nazi-occupied France. Even today, despite the presence of new ski resorts, the inevitable desecration of power lines and the modern roads that traverse the remote valleys or tunnel their way through its impassable heights, the Pyrenees have preserved its sense of apartness.

All this high country is the home of eagles and vultures, most notably the lammergeier, or bearded vulture. In Spanish, this enormous raptor is known as *quebrantahuesos* – the bone-breaker – due to its unique feeding habit of dropping animal carcasses on the rocks to get at the marrow. Here, too, in the remotest valleys, the brown bear lingers like a legend. But the isard, the Pyrenean version of the chamois, is common everywhere, and we watched them picking their way across perilous ledges with no regard for the void beneath.

At first there had seemed to be no way out of the Circo de Soaso. We watched braver souls heading off through a defile in the direction of *Las Clavijas* – a set of iron pegs hammered into the cliffs by a 19th-century ibex hunter – but they called for the nerves of a tightrope walker. Then we spotted the faintest trace of a path zigzagging up precipitous aprons of scree to a crag where hands as well as feet were needed to gain access to the easier slopes above.

That night we stayed at the Góriz mountain refuge, dining cheaply and well on rabbit stew, and sharing a three-tiered dormitory with 70 snoring Spaniards. The room was warm, but the air was thick enough to cut with a cheese wire and we were glad to be on our way next morning.

Now the last of the limestone pastures lay behind us. We toiled on past lonely tarns covered with a skin of ice, into a lunar wasteland of frost-shattered rock. Above us, glaciers glinted against the sky as we passed beneath Monte Perdido – the lost mountain. Somewhere a raven grunted, and its guttural voice was taken up in the silence and flung, echoing, from crag to crag. Ahead rose the savage summits that run like watchtowers along the spine of Europe's wildest frontier – the triple peaks of Marboré, the crooked gables of Pico Taillon. And in between, like a missing tooth, a gap in the intervening crest of the hundred-metre cliffs called the Brèche de Roland.

Roland was the paladin killed by the Basques as he fought to secure the safe withdrawal of Charlemagne's forces across the Pyrenees. His death at Roncesvalles (nowhere near the Brèche de

Roland) became the stuff of legend. The Basques became Saracens and Roland a giant with a magic sword, Durandel. With his dying strength, Roland struck the mountain, trying in vain to break his sword so that it would not fall into the hands of his enemies. The result was the Brèche, the natural gateway for mountain walkers passing between Spain and France.

It was while resting at this spot that I came as close to death as I have ever been. While taking a breather after our long ascent I had been vaguely aware of two climbers scaling the vertical walls of the Brèche. For some reason I stepped forward a couple of paces, and as I did so a slab of rock the size of a grand piano landed with a sickening thud exactly where I had been standing a second ago. Dislodged by the climbers above us, it would have killed me instantly.

Mountains are sacred places and sometimes they give rise to profound thoughts. I remembered that I had undertaken this walk as a rite of passage, a midlife challenge to celebrate the passing of a significant birthday. Now, notwithstanding my brush with mortality in the portals of the Brèche, with one foot in Spain and the other in France, it occurred to me that I was poised on the roof of my life.

Behind me lay the ground I had covered, and all the mountains of Spain fading away in five distinct ranges (one for each decade, I thought) to the infinity of the horizon. Ahead to the north lay the mountains of France, hazy and indistinct in the September sunshine. Somewhere down there, beyond the snowfields that sloped around this wide upper lip of the Cirque de Gavarnie, was the promise of dinner, a hot bath, and clean sheets in Luz-Saint-Sauveur.

It was growing colder. I took one last look into the golden haze of Spain, then turned and walked down through the snow to begin the rest of my life.

CHAPTER EIGHTEEN

IN January 1986, life at the *Sunday Times* went from bad to worse when nearly 6,000 newspaper workers went on strike following the collapse of talks on Murdoch's plans to move News International's operations to a new plant at Wapping in East London's Dockland.

Like most British newspapers, the *Sunday Times* was still produced using hot-metal typesetting, a process that had been in operation since the late 19th century. Murdoch wanted to introduce new technology, but the print unions refused to budge. The bitter dispute that followed lasted until February 1987 and we journalists were caught up in the middle at what become known as Fortress Wapping, surrounded by razor wire, mounted police and striking printers yelling 'scab, scab, scab' at anyone crossing the picket lines. In the end, Murdoch won. The print unions had no option but to accept News International's redundancy terms and Fleet Street would never be the same again.

At least I was able to escape from the soulless surroundings of Fortress Wapping on various stories for the magazine or pieces for the travel pages, and one assignment in particular turned out to be one of the most satisfying I had ever undertaken.

Sixty years had passed since Henry Williamson wrote *Tarka the Otter*, still regarded as the greatest nature classic in the English language, and 1987 was the year of his centenary. On this flimsy pretext I persuaded the magazine to release me from Dockland's dreary clutches and returned to Tarka's Devon, transporting me as

Williamson's immortal tale had done so often for me when I was growing up.

Henry Williamson was born in London in 1895. In 1914 he joined the army and fought in the trenches on the Western Front until, traumatically, he was sent home badly gassed and shell-shocked.

After the war he worked in London as a freelance journalist, but city life proved too much for his shattered nerves. In 1921 he climbed on to his 499cc BRS Norton motorbike and roared off to build a new life in North Devon.

In the village of Georgeham, for 18 pence a week he rented a cob-and-thatch labourer's dwelling where he lived for years with no companions except dogs and cats – and at one stage an orphaned otter cub. Williamson persuaded his cat to suckle the cub, and as it grew up it would follow him on long walks around the countryside. But one evening it stepped in a gin trap. By the time Williamson managed to release it, the trap had almost severed three of its toes. In fright, the animal wriggled from his grasp and vanished. He never saw the otter again but the idea of Tarka had been born.

More than any other writer since Thomas Hardy, Williamson's lyrical prose caught the spirit of a special corner of England and made it his own. Williamson country lies between Exmoor and Dartmoor where two Devon rivers, the Taw and Torridge, emerge from their deep wooded valleys to meet the Atlantic in a vast estuary of salt marsh, dunes, and sandbars. Williamson walked and loved every inch of it and described it so faithfully that, even in the 1980s, with a decent map and a copy of Tarka, I could follow his footsteps across the printed page.

'Tarka's fame irritated Henry,' said Daniel Farson, Williamson's biographer, whom I met in Appledore. 'Yet he was also immensely proud of it.' Farson, who was still in his teens when they first met, remembered him in those days as 'a lean, vibrant, almost quivering man with blazing mesmeric eyes'.

'They were idyllic days,' said Farson, describing the golden summers of the late 1940s. Yet even as early as 1953, as Farson's biography of Williamson records, Henry was already lamenting the changes which had overtaken the North Devon coast around Appledore. 'Paper, Wall's ice cream cartons, shrieking children. A polluted estuary. A £1 million electric coal station erected just over the water on the snipe bogs that once were. The Burrows are a tank ground now.'

In the 1920s Williamson could still write about the 'wild, beautiful, unexplored Atlantic seaboard; the falcons, the badgers, the otters, the salmon, the character of the people', as if Devon was another country. Farmers in early spring would stamp out into the soft West Country dawns to plough their fields with heavy horses, just as I had done when evacuated to Cornwall; and pigs were killed outside cottage doors, squealing as their blood poured into bowls for 'bloody pie'.

In Appledore, among the cobbled alleys and sawdust-smelling boatyards, you might still have found old 'mast-and-yards' men who had served their sea time aboard square-rigged sailing ships; and it was not uncommon even then to see a three-masted schooner waiting for the flood tide to carry her up to Bideford.

Williamson was writing in the sunset of English rural life. In the villages, the old order, shaken to its roots by the Great War, would never be the same. A land that had never moved faster than the pace of a horse was being laid open by railways and metalled roads. New bridges and viaducts brought the green-and-gold locomotives of the Southern Railway steaming down the valleys from Exeter, 40 miles away, and motor cars – a rare sight in the 1920s – became commonplace in the lanes.

The way of life that Williamson described had been laid to rest. Yet echoes, places, ghosts remained. The settings were much the same and it was only when you compared his vivid descriptions with the reality of the present that it was possible to measure the changes which had overtaken, and in places overwhelmed, North Devon.

Those were the days when you could walk down to the estuary and be rowed across to Appledore for a shilling. Now it was all holiday coast. Saunton and Putsborough Sands surrendered long ago to the surfers and sunbathers, and in summer the lanes were choked with traffic heading for the beaches. In Tarka's day the mouth of the Yeo was wedged between green fields and Monkey Island. Now the island lay buried beneath Barnstaple's multi-storey civic centre. Only Baggy Point remained untouched – a wild National Trust headland where the Atlantic bursts with gasping force against lichen-scabbed cliffs.

To the south lay Dartmoor, now protected as a national park, where the Taw rises among desolate bogs under Hangingstone Hill. In its upper reaches the Taw is a typical Dartmoor stream, spilling over mossy boulders in a chain of amber pools. Downstream below King's Nympton, diesel trains rumbled over iron bridges that Williamson knew in the age of steam; but here at least in the lush farmlands the Taw was timeless. It remained the 'Gentlemen's River' – so-called by the old otter hunters who knew that wherever they stopped for midday refreshments they would never be far from a riverside inn.

Nowhere in Devon is Williamson's presence closer than on the banks of the Torridge. For much of its 50 odd miles, especially in its upper reaches above Torrington, it is a secret river. Sometimes, cruising down the back lanes that criss-cross this part of the county, you catch a tantalising glimpse of it, sliding like polished glass under bankside oaks, or running bright over stony shillets between summertime jungles of pink Himalayan balsam. But most of the time it shuns the road, losing itself in the woods and water meadows of a landscape unchanged since Williamson's time.

Now, as then, what the visitor sees is a time-warp countryside of herons and buttercups, in which Beam Weir and Halfpenny Bridge – familiar scenes in Tarka – remain just as they were when the book was written. Even vanished landmarks had been brought back to life. Below Canal Bridge, near Weare Giffard, 13 gnarled trees once stood with their roots in the river. In one was Owlery Holt, Tarka's birthplace. All had gone, but 13 new trees now stood in their place, planted by the Tarka Project, a Devon County Council initiative designed to promote sustainable tourism in the region by creating a 180-mile 'Tarka Trail' footpath.

In Williamson's day, of course, otter hunting was still popular, as he vividly describes in his account of Tarka's battle with Deadlock, the great pied hound of the Two Rivers. But otter hunting had been banned in 1977, allowing the species to recover from the lethal effects of pesticides that had almost brought about their extinction.

It would have been foolish to imagine that North Devon had not changed in half a century, or that life was better in Williamson's day. Roads, housing estates, power lines and pollution had all conspired to diminish its beauty. Yet the 'Land of the Two Rivers' remained its own place, stubborn and inward-looking. And all because a shell-shocked survivor from the trenches sought refuge there with an orphaned otter cub and gave it immortality.

****

Not all my assignments turned out to be as idyllic as my sojourn in Tarka territory. One of the first people I met on my first visit to East Africa was Dr Iain Douglas-Hamilton, the world's leading elephant zoologist. Since then, he had been at the forefront of efforts to halt the illegal ivory trade that was decimating Africa's elephant herds. 'Make no mistake,' he had warned, 'what we are witnessing in Africa is the greatest animal tragedy of this century.'

For years, the price of ivory had remained stable at around £1 per pound. In 1969 prices had suddenly tripled and in 1972 they tripled again – almost a tenfold increase in three years. The boom was almost certainly engineered by a few big international dealers holding back their stocks so that, overnight, ivory became a commodity like gold, to be salted away in a bank vault as a hedge against inflation.

The word had spread swiftly to the poachers in the bush and the ivory rush was on. From Kenya the illegal trade spread rapidly into neighbouring Uganda and Tanzania and then on until it reached into every part of the elephant's range.

Because of my growing involvement with Africa, I had begun to report on the increasingly vicious struggle to save the elephant from extinction, and in 1988 I was despatched by the *Sunday Times Magazine* to the killing fields of Kenya, where the poaching epidemic had transformed Tsavo from the country's biggest national park into an elephant graveyard.

Tsavo is classic elephant country. Its sheer size – though a nightmare to patrol – is also its greatest strength and here, it was hoped, the herds might wander freely and at peace. Sadly, that was not to be. By the 1960s their numbers had swelled to around 35,000, giving rise to demands that they should be culled to save the park's vegetation from destruction; but the savage five-year drought that ravaged Tsavo in the early 1970s put paid to that. By the time it was over more than 9,000 elephants had died, and as the price of ivory soared, the survivors became a prime target for the poachers.

In the beginning the main culprits were the Waliangulu, a small tribe of hunter-gatherers also known as the 'People of the Longbow', whose bows were more powerful than those used by the English at Agincourt, and whose arrows – fletched with vulture feathers – were dipped in a lethal tarry substance brewed from the *Acokanthera* shrub for which there is no antidote.

The Waliangulu in turn were ruthlessly displaced by the *shifta* – heavily armed poaching gangs who swept down from Somalia. Their weapon of choice was the AK-47 and the elephants died in the thousands. By 1988 large areas of Tsavo were considered too dangerous for tourists and placed off limits as soldiers, police and anti-poaching patrols engaged the Somali ivory gangs in bloody skirmishes.

So dangerous had the situation become that Tsavo had been declared out of bound to journalists, but I went anyway. Smuggled in with the help of a sympathetic ranger and accompanied by a fearless local conservationist called Marcus Russell, I sneaked into the park to look for evidence of the slaughter which had resulted in at least 500 elephants being killed by poachers in the previous six months.

It was the vultures that gave the game away. Dozens of them, hunched in the leafless trees like obscene fruit. As we drew closer the dry, pure air of Tsavo was poisoned by the gut-churning stench of death.

There were six carcasses. All had been small elephants and they had fallen where the poachers had surprised them, on their way to drink at a waterhole. One had collapsed in a kneeling position, its huge ears still spread as in life, a grotesque parody of an elephant with its trunk cut off and its tusks chopped out.

I could see the holes where the poachers' bullets had struck. They had been dead only two weeks but a fortnight in the sun had reduced them to shrunken tents of red hide, splashed by vulture droppings, and hollowed by hyenas.

A week later the same gang killed another six elephants 20 kilometres away, but this time their luck ran out. As they made for their hideout in the Kulalu hills they were spotted from the air by Joe Kioko, the park's acting head warden. Within 20 minutes his anti-poaching patrols were in pursuit and, in the gun battle which followed, two poachers were shot dead and three captured. All were Somalis.

Although some poaching was being carried out with the connivance of corrupt park officials the great mass of killings were the work of the *shifta* and their work was all too plain to see in the gruesome clusters of corpses we found, where whole elephant families had been gunned down.

In three days, I counted 35 carcasses, all with their tusks hacked out, every one of them killed in the previous six weeks. One animal, although hit eight times, had managed to hobble away, dragging a shattered leg across 400 metres of rocky ground, only to die within a few metres of the river it had been trying to reach. Another, a cow elephant, had been shot in the act of giving birth and lay with her dead calf beside her.

As for live elephants, the park appeared utterly deserted. From the Yatta Plateau to Mtito Andei and all the way down to Mudanda Rock I saw none. Worse still, there was no sign of the giant footprints, no green boulders of dung left in the roads by the wandering herds.

Only an occasional bleached bone, too big even for the hyenas to break open, to hint at the tragedy being enacted.

Only when I followed the Voi River down to the Kanderi swamp did I find them. There, miraculously, a herd of about 150 had gathered to feed on the lush swamp grasses. As I watched, more elephants came marching in until there were perhaps 350 all feeding peacefully. 'Enjoy it while you can,' said Marcus. 'You're looking at about 30 per cent of what's left of the East Tsavo herds.'

It was primarily to protect these huge migratory gatherings that Tsavo had been created in 1948. Its 13,671 square miles of arid bush were of little use to man, but to the elephants it held out the best hope of survival in a shrinking world. Here they could still wander freely across the vast, dusty face of Africa. At least, that was the dream. I saw no more elephants that day, but all the way down the road to the Sala Gate I passed bones and skulls – all missing their tusks – where the poachers had been busy.

For Kenya's thriving, wildlife-based tourist industry – worth at least £200 million a year at that time – this was a disaster. Kill the elephants, scare away the tourists and the country's economy would lie in ruins.

It was therefore with some dismay that conservationists heard George Muhoho, Kenya's minister for wildlife and tourism, claim improved efficiency in protecting the herds. He expressed 'regrets' over the killings but assured his audience that the parks were safe for visitors.

This was too much for Richard Leakey, the distinguished palaeontologist and chairman of the East African Wildlife Society, who unleashed a furious attack on Muhoho's failure to control the poaching.

Next day Muhoho struck back, claiming that Kenya still had 22,000 elephants; but Leakey was not to be silenced. The figure of 22,000, he said, was 'misleading'. At the end of the previous year there were no more than 20,000 elephants and possibly a great many fewer. Then he dropped his bombshell. The minister, he said, had already received a confidential list naming people inside his own ministry who were involved in poaching. The document had been presented to Muhoho more than a month earlier and had been gathering dust ever since.

Muhoho's only response was to denounce Leakey for his 'cheeky white mentality', implying – quite wrongly – that it was only Kenya's expatriate community who were concerned about protecting wildlife.

For Muhoho, a former Catholic priest and the brother of President Kenyatta's widow, Mama Ngina, it was a disastrous performance. But at least the acrimonious exchange with Leakey had put the crisis on centre stage.

Meanwhile the poachers were becoming even bolder. In September a tourist was shot and wounded when bandits held up and robbed a safari minibus in Meru National Park. Two months later they returned to Meru and killed Kenya's only five white rhinos in their enclosure.

For President Moi this was the last straw. Having already authorised a shoot-to-kill policy to combat the poachers, he now appointed Richard Leakey as Kenya's new director of National Parks.

At last the tide was beginning to turn. In 1989 President Moi would put a torch to more than a hundred tonnes of tusks when Kenya publicly burnt its ivory stocks, sending a message that went around the world; and in 1990, after Leakey had created the Kenya Wildlife Service as a paramilitary force to wipe out the poaching gangs, CITES – the Convention on International Trade in Endangered Species – would finally come to its senses and ban the international ivory trade.

The killing and the illegal trade it fed would continue for years to come with no end in sight, but at least the species now had a chance to avoid extinction. My story was published in the *Sunday Times Magazine*, spread over half a dozen pages under the banner headline: 'Kenya's bloody ivory', and I was proud to have played a small part in bringing public opinion to bear on the survival of Africa's remaining elephant herds.

****

Nevertheless, reporting on Africa's ivory wars did not come without risks. It was around this time that I began to research a story on South Africa's illegal ivory trade. Over the years I had built up an invaluable network of contacts who kept me informed with what was happening in the battle to save Africa's elephants and rhinos.

Foremost among them was Esmond Bradley Martin, a fearless New Yorker who had moved to Britain in 1970 to take a PhD in geography at Liverpool and arrived in Kenya soon after, just at the time when the elephant holocaust was beginning to take off. By then he had already begun working with Chryssee, his wife, to write *Cargoes of the East*, a history of the dhow trade between East Africa and the Gulf.

Inevitably, Bradley Martin began to pick up the rumours circulating in Mombasa and Lamu; how consignments of elephant tusks were being smuggled out of Africa, hidden at the bottom of ocean-going dhows under piles of mangrove poles. At the same time, he discovered how new-found wealth from Middle East oil was fuelling an unprecedented demand for rhino horns in the Yemen, where they are prized as handles for *jambiyas* (traditional curved daggers). Snappily dressed like Tom Wolfe in a cream linen suit, a silk handkerchief spilling from his breast pocket and his silver hair flopping over his forehead, Esmond Bradley Martin looked more like a literary critic than the sworn enemy of the illegal trade in ivory and rhino horn. He was a man with impeccable manners and a fondness for string quartets and antebellum architecture. But beneath that deceptively fey exterior he was as tough as teak and totally fearless as he worked undercover, posing as a buyer to expose the smuggling cartels and their international trafficking routes between Africa and southeast Asia.

Bent customs officials, crooked politicians, dodgy dealers, and their middlemen – nobody was safe from his cloak-and-dagger investigations. Not even ambassadors who exported rhino horns in their diplomatic bags, or the official at the Italian embassy in Lusaka whom he fingered for trying to smuggle ivory out of Zambia in a sack of dog meat.

The deeper he dug into the booming trade in wildlife products the more he became determined to devote his life to staunching the flow of horns and tusks that was bleeding Africa dry. By now he had also met up with Iain Douglas-Hamilton, who had been among the first to create an international outcry at the poachers' massive onslaught on Africa's dwindling elephant herds, and the two men had worked together for the next 18 years.

I first got to know Esmond when I was exposing the slaughter of elephants in Tsavo, and without his help I could have never unravelled the web of corruption that reached up into the highest echelons of President Moi's government.

Whenever he came to London we would always meet up, not at the Knightsbridge Green Hotel where he always stayed, but at a greasy-spoon café in the Gray's Inn Road. Here over a cup of tea and a bacon sarnie, he would drip-feed me the latest revelations he had managed to extract from his regular visits to the remote and dangerous international hotspots where the illegal ivory cartels plied their trade.

'Esmond was one of conservation's great unsung champions,' said Iain Douglas-Hamilton, 'meticulously gathering data on the world's ivory and rhino horn markets with no care for his personal safety.'

It therefore came as no surprise when he was stabbed to death in his Nairobi home in February 2018. He had just returned from an investigative trip to Myanmar, yet another destination that had fallen under his spotlight for its associations with the illegal wildlife trade. Those responsible for his murder were never caught. Nor was the motive ever conclusively established; but his achievements are there for all to see wherever elephants continue to roam in Africa's parks and wildlife strongholds.

On this occasion, however, the tip-off about South Africa's involvement in illegal ivory trading had come from the Environmental Investigation Agency, a highly respected international NGO based in London and Washington.

The EIA was founded in 1984 by Dave Currey, a minister's son who had walked a thousand miles across the USA in 1976 to raise awareness of conservation issues for the World Wildlife Fund. In 1979 he joined the Greenpeace ship *Rainbow Warrior* as a volunteer during its anti-whaling campaigns and met Allan Thornton, Greenpeace's director, who teamed up with Currey to spearhead the EIA's investigative campaigns. Very soon they had become the wildlife equivalent of the CIA, covertly identifying the transnational criminal groups involved in everything from logging to ivory and exposing their trade routes from Africa to the Far East.

Currey was the source of several environmental features I had written for the *Sunday Times Magazine* on various topics from tiger conservation to Senegal's illegal trade in wild birds; so, when he approached me to talk about South Africa's involvement in the ivory racket, I knew we were on to a scoop.

For nearly 30 years the country had been subjected to a UN arms embargo, and its apartheid regime was desperately trying to cling to power by any means, including sanctions-busting schemes whereby ivory was being illegally exchanged for arms and other much-needed commodities. The result, said Currey, was that tusks were pouring in from all over Africa and making their way to Pretoria, where the Poon Brothers, two of Hong Kong's most notorious ivory traders, kept their warehouses.

That was the story, and we knew we were on to something big when Peter Godwin, the paper's South African stringer, had his Cape Town flat trashed. Clearly it was a warning. Drop the story. We were getting too close to the truth and the individuals involved did not want the rest of the world to know about their dirty little secret. Of course, to an investigative paper like the *Sunday Times*, that was like waving a red rag at a bull, and only caused us to redouble our efforts.

The next thing I knew was that I was called up to the editor's office to be told that they had received a phone call from MI5, saying a hitman had been sent from South Africa to prevent the story getting out. My first feeling was one of disbelief. I was just a travel writer, working for the soft underbelly of the paper, and dramas of this kind simply never happened to people like me. But there was no doubt the threat was serious because I was given a bodyguard.

The man I was introduced to was smartly dressed in a grey two-piece suit and Guards' tie, but it soon became apparent that he was a former member of the SAS. 'Tell me exactly which route you take home when leaving the office,' he said. 'I'll be keeping you in plain sight all the time, even if you don't see me. And if you do, please don't acknowledge me in any way.'

Meanwhile, one of Murdoch's security staff was sent down to Dorset to look after my wife and daughter in our remote rural cottage.

I left the office at around 6pm, walked down the Gray's Inn Road and caught the tube from Kings Cross to Ladbroke Grove as I always did when sharing a flat during the working week with Lawrence Gordon Clark, an old friend of mine whose home was in Cornwall but who worked for Yorkshire Television.

I sat down in the tube and saw my bodyguard at the other end of the carriage and noticed the polished leather case on his lap – the same one he had when I met him – and presumed that it concealed an automatic weapon.

That night, when I looked out of my upstairs window, cautiously easing back the curtains an inch or two, there was no sign of him; but there was a van parked outside I had never seen before, with someone in the driver's seat.

The same routine happened every day that week until Sunday, when the story made front-page news. I never saw my bodyguard again and can only presume that once the exposé had been published my would-be assassin was recalled and normal life resumed.

PART THREE

THE GIRL WITH THE NORTH SEA EYES

'To wake at dawn to the song of the lion is to breathe the air of a vanishing freedom.'

From *Savannah Diaries* (Bradt, 2014)

CHAPTER NINETEEN

EARLIER in 1988, in March to be precise, I found myself at work on another *Sunday Times Magazine* story that could not have been more different from the adrenaline high of reporting from the front line in the fight to save the elephant.

In East Anglia the parish church, the pillar of the rural establishment and centrepiece of every village, was in trouble. Old age, falling congregations and rising damp had all conspired to create a crisis of faith in the countryside. So it was that in early spring, just after the clocks had gone forward, I found myself with freelance photographer Richard Dudley-Smith in rural Norfolk.

There, church towers still beckoned across the fields, each one a prayer in stone and flint offered up to God by its medieval builders, unlettered men with calloused hands and an unswerving faith that what they had created would stand for all eternity.

The miracle, perhaps, is that so many had survived for so long, frail geriatrics tottering uncertainly towards the last decade of the 20th century. Now time was catching up with them. Damp English winters were taking their toll. Gutters became clogged. Nail-sick roofs let in the rain. Dry rot extended its greedy fingers and death-watch beetles turned great beams to dust.

In the two previous decades more than 1,200 of Britain's 16,000 parish churches had been declared redundant. In nearly every parish God's acre was under siege; but nowhere was the problem of neglected country churches greater than in Norfolk.

At Tunstall, on the edge of the Halvergate Marshes, we stopped to visit the Church of St Peter and St Paul. Once its bells had rung out every Sunday across the marshland fields. Now their tumbling voices were stilled for ever. The church was a roofless ruin with just one end preserved. There were jackdaws in the tower, nettles in the nave. On the wooden lectern, beside pews spattered with bird droppings, a prayer book lay open at the *Nunc Dimittis*, the evening prayer.

Not far away at Runham stood what was then another noble wreck, a lonely marshland church foundering like a stricken galleon in a sea of corn. Two of the stone pinnacles from its lofty Perpendicular-style tower had been cast down; and propped against the porch was a warning sign in large red letters: DANGEROUS BUILDING – *keep out*.

It is part of Norfolk's glory that it can boast the highest density of churches in Europe.

Their flint towers dominate the wide horizons. Many are round towers from the time of the Conquest. Rooted in the landscape like ancient trees, the oldest may have seen the Normans with their chain-mail coats and kite-shaped shields, marching north to fight Hereward in the Fens, and some are less than a mile apart. At Reepham, two churches stand cheek by jowl in the same churchyard.

Not all are spectacular but 659 are medieval. Symbols of wealth and pride no less than faith, built in a golden age of wool and weaving. But when the wool trade receded, the churches were left stranded, godforsaken among the fields.

Such was the church we went to find in the village of Forncett St Mary, marooned in the flatlands between Diss and Wymondham. Richard was keen to photograph it, but already the light was beginning to fail.

As we entered the village, I noticed a young woman by the roadside, and we stopped to ask her the way to the church. I was vaguely aware that she was wearing a khaki boiler suit and green wellies, but what struck me about her was her direct gaze. Although it was a cool spring evening, I suddenly found myself shivering uncontrollably, and as I looked into her grey North Sea eyes, I felt my heart turn over.

Was this the result of pheromones at their mysterious work? The French have a phrase for it: *un coup de foudre* – literally a thunderbolt; but in any language it translates as love at first sight.

She was standing at the entrance to a rather grand Victorian mansion with a letter in her hand. We had met just as she was on her way to the village postbox. Her name was Annabelle, she said, and offered to guide us to where the church stood not far away.

While Richard was busy taking pictures, I walked back with her to the spot where we had first met. Beside the entrance to the mansion stood a board, stating that this was Forncett Manor, a retirement home whose proprietor was Annabelle Pritt.

It was a former *Sunday Times* colleague, Nick Tomalin, who is credited with the immortal phrase: 'The only qualities essential for real success in journalism are rat-like cunning and a plausible manner', and now was the time to put his advice into practice. At the foot of the board was a telephone number which I furtively scribbled down while thanking her in what I hoped was a plausible manner that even Nick himself would have approved of.

It has often occurred to me since that day how fate so often determines our future. Had we not driven through the village precisely at that moment, or had she chosen to post her letter sometime later, our lives would have been changed utterly – rather like the film

Sliding Doors, in which John Hannah and Gwyneth Paltrow would never have met but for one brief inconsequential moment.

At this point I should explain that back home in Powerstock my marriage had finally run out of steam. Understandably, although both of us had deliberately chosen to exchange suburban Surrey for a greener life in rural Dorset, Sarah was becoming increasingly unhappy at being left at home with our daughter while I was commuting to London or else flying off to exotic destinations for the *Sunday Times'* travel pages. We still laughed together and spent time with our West Bay friends at weekends, but the spark was no longer there. It was only Imogen's presence that kept us together; but she was no longer a child, having metamorphosed into a beautiful teenager who would soon leave the nest.

Like those of many men, my social antennae have never been very perceptive, but eventually I began to suspect that Sarah was finding solace elsewhere. At weekends, when I was outdoors, she would leave a note on the table, saying: 'I'm just going shopping; I may be some little time.' In the end it almost became a mantra and one day, feeling terribly guilty for doubting her word, I checked the mileage on the car before she drove off. Bridport, our nearest shopping centre, was only three miles away, but when I checked the mileage on her return there were an extra 20 miles on the clock.

All the clues pointed to the fact that – to coin a phrase – somebody had been rumpling the duvet while I was away, and her indiscretions were now taking place even while I was at home. But who? Eventually it turned out to be a friend I had known for 20 years, an artist who had never married but was seldom without an attractive partner for long.

I decided that discretion was the best course of action, if only for the sake of our daughter. Besides, in time it might all blow over; but I also vowed that if anyone else turned up in my life as Annabelle had done, I would not let the opportunity pass by.

For the time being, though, I conducted our courtship at long distance, by letter and by phone. I found that we had much in common, including a shared love of simple things: cuckoos and cow parsley and orange-tip butterflies; and most surprising of all for someone I found so irresistibly attractive, she had never married.

Over the next few months, I also discovered that she was born in Aldeburgh on the Suffolk coast, where her father owned the Wentworth Hotel until he died in 1983. There she had grown up with her three sisters and brother Michael, who now ran the hotel.

After leaving home she had travelled right across North America and down to Mexico and back on a shoestring budget, using a special deal offered by Greyhound buses that offered 99 days' unlimited travel for $99. Back in England again, she embarked on a successful career as a nursing sister in Great Yarmouth before becoming frustrated with the bureaucracy of the NHS, after which she had gone into business with a nursing colleague. Together they had bought the derelict manor house in Forncett St Mary where we had met and had transformed it into a gracious retirement home.

****

For the time being, though, romance was on hold. My journalistic career carried on as before, and in May I fulfilled a long-held dream of visiting the Isles of Scilly.

Although only 28 miles from Land's End, they lie out in the Gulf Stream where frosts are rare, and sunfish bask in summer. There are no snakes, no mosquitoes, no muggers, and if you took the helicopter from Penzance you could be there in 20 minutes.

The chopper touched down in a daisy field, as lightly as a gull on a roof, and I stepped out into a luminous, sea-girt world that looked like the Cornwall of 60 years ago. I breathed deeply, drinking in the salty Scillonian air. Distilled by crossing 4,000 miles of Atlantic Ocean, these same breezes brought unusual and exotic birds to the islands: nighthawks and magnolia warblers from America, hoopoes, and golden orioles from southern Europe.

While the rest of Britain shivers in the grip of winter, the Scillonians are busy in their pocket-sized bulb fields, cutting daffodils for the London market. By the time I arrived, parts of the islands were as luxuriant as the Mediterranean. Palm trees sprouted from cottage gardens, and bees droned among giant azure spires of echiums from the Canaries. On St Mary's, the main island, I saw a blue field, like a Picasso painting: a solid carpet of Spanish bluebells. Other fields were bright with Bermuda buttercups and Whistling Jacks – wild red gladioli from Africa once grown commercially but now gone native, rooted among the more familiar West Country flowers.

It made me think. When my roving days were over, maybe I, too, should put down my roots here, in a granite cottage, snug under the sea wind, with a garden full of daffodils and a view of the sea as blue as the Caribbean; and on Bryher I met someone who had done just that.

Mac Mace was the man I had come to interview, a professional diver from Nottingham who had successfully transplanted himself on this, the smallest of Scilly's five inhabited islands, where he and Tracy, his wife, ran a guesthouse.

The sea began at his garden gate. From his lounge he could point out the sites of 22 shipwrecks. Indoors he proudly showed me a brass signal cannon he had retrieved from the wreck of Admiral Sir Cloudesley Shovell's flagship, HMS *Association*. 'Possibly the last gun she fired before she struck on the Gilstone Ledge on a stormy October night in 1707,' said Mace.

'She was a 90-gun ship of the line and she was carrying the Queen's plate, 10 chests of Sir Cloudesley's own and great riches of the grandees of Spain. Now she is lying in a 30-metre-deep valley, scattered across a seabed of cottage-sized boulders. You can see the snouts of her cannons, but the gold and silver and other artefacts have dribbled down between the rocks,' he said, 'and getting at them is more like mining than diving.'

Yet, little by little, the *Association* had been yielding up her treasure: English silver coins welded together by centuries of corrosion; Portuguese gold pieces as bright as the day they were minted. The previous year Mace had found an apricot stone which he almost persuaded to germinate, and, most poignant of all, a seaman's gold ring inscribed with the words: 'In thy breast my heart does rest.'

On a sunny day, the waters around Bryher are idyllic, a maze of ledges and gull-haunted islets threaded by glittering turquoise channels. One such stretch has the most beautiful name in all Scilly: the Garden of Maiden Bower. But how different it is in a big winter storm when Hell Bay seethes like scalded milk and the roaring seas break clean over the outlying rock castles of Mincarlo.

Mac Mace knew well the unimaginable power of the sea. Once he dived on the ill-fated tanker *Torrey Canyon*, wrecked on the Seven

Stones reef in 1967. 'She's huge, an 11-storey hull of solid iron,' he said. 'Yet the sea had shoved her along the bottom for more than a hundred metres since she went down.'

He was equally knowledgeable about Bryher, knew every inch of its 134 hectares of yellow gorse and Iron Age cairns. 'Look,' he cried, sinking to his knees to identify a blue pinhead in the grass. It turned out to be a rare miniature violet which, he said, grew only here and in the Channel Islands.

'People come to Bryher and ask us what there is to do, and we tell them there's nothing. That is the joy of it, that and the sense of man having lived here for 3,000 years.'

On Bryher, as elsewhere in the Scillies, such joys are synonymous with peace and tranquillity. Even on St Mary's where locals were complaining about the island's 300 cars, traffic has a minimal presence. Boats are far more important, and every morning a stream of launches sets out from St Mary's Quay to deposit visitors on the smaller islands for the day.

On Tresco, the most popular of the off-islands, I wandered around the sub-tropical gardens of Tresco Abbey and came upon their extraordinary Valhalla of shipwrecked figureheads. Gilded and ghostly white, they flew out of the shadows as if they were still cleaving the wild Atlantic. There were golden lions, blue dolphins, a Highland chief, and a Puritan maid. But the loveliest and most enigmatic by far was a brown-eyed lass with a comb in her hair – the Spanish lady – salvaged from a mystery vessel dashed upon the Scilly Rocks.

Back in Hugh Town on St Mary's, I bought a wreck chart of the Scillies produced by Roland Morris of Penzance, every inch of it littered with the names of dead ships: barques and brigantines, East Indiamen and ships of the line, clippers bound to Falmouth for orders, Dutch galliots, French crabbers, proud schooners, and humble steam trawlers. A chilling document – a roll call of the deep – showing the hundreds of ships lost and men drowned in these islands over the centuries.

It lists cargoes of fustic and indigo, tea from Foochow, coal from Cardiff, and each terse entry tells a story. The ship *Palinurus* on passage from Demerara to London with rum and sugar, lost with all hands... the SS *Schiller*, wrecked on the Retarrier Ledges with the loss of more than 300 lives... the *Louisa Hannah* returning from Lisbon, laden with oranges and wine on her way home to Poole, lost with all hands off Annet in 1839.

And listen to the names of the rocks that sent them crashing to the bottom: Tearing Ledge, the Hellweathers, Great Wingletang, the Gunners, the Beast, and the infamous Gilstone.

> *Who sank the Association?*
> *I, said the Gilstone,*
> *She sank like a millstone.*

Next day I went out to the Western Rocks to visit some of those unrepentant old murderers. The boat rose and fell among the hills of blue water. Shell-bursts of spray blossomed against the Haycocks, too far away to hear, and the Bishop Rock lighthouse stood pencil-slim on its solitary pinnacle like an admonishing finger. What courage it must have taken to live there, marooned among those fearsome deeps, knowing the first lighthouse to be built on the Bishop was washed away in a storm.

Puffins whirred from beneath our bows, and grey seals with sleek mottled bodies and wistful eyes slipped into the water as we nosed among the reefs of Rosevean and Melledgen. Even on a calm day the sea is never still. The tide sucks constantly at the barnacled granite, swilling around the teeth and tusks of those grim ledges to subside with a sinister gasp, like the last breath of a drowning sailor. You think of all the fine ships that have come to grief here, and the sunless silence of the kelp forests below, and pray the weather holds.

On my last morning, as cloudless as the first, I rented a bike in Hugh Town and went freewheeling down the empty lanes to the sea. The day stretched before me and I felt as carefree as a child. Where the road ended, I left the bike among the bluebells, knowing nobody would steal it, and set out along the coast path to Porth Hellick. The scent of the gorse rolled in thick coconut tides across the cliff tops. The sea lay glassy calm. Out on the horizon beyond Great Arthur a faint smudge of a ship caught my eye. I stared at it through my binoculars in disbelief. It was a ghost ship, a dream ship from the past: a great square-rigger under sail.

That evening she lay at anchor in the tideway known as St Mary's Road. She was the *Belem*, a French sail-training ship homeward bound for Nantes. But for me, her masts and shrouds deep-etched against the dying golden light, she was a haunting echo from a century ago when these perilous waters were the crossroads of the world and the swift, six-oared Scillonian pilot gigs – *Shah, Bonnet, Golden Eagle* – rowed out between the Western Rocks to guide the tall ships safely home.

CHAPTER TWENTY

THE Fens of East Anglia, deep-drained and embanked against the tide, are one of the most mysterious places in Britain. Their open skies and wide horizons reflect an epic chapter in the making of the English landscape. They contain some of the richest land anywhere in Europe and yet they are haunted by the fear of their oldest enemy – the rising sea.

Never was this fear more apparent in recent times than on 25th January 1990, when the great hurricane that came to be known as the Burns' Day Storm swept across southern Britain, felling thousands of trees and killing scores of people before rampaging on across the North Sea.

The level fields of Cambridgeshire were freshly stitched with winter wheat. Brimming dykes ran out to the horizon. Ely Cathedral, the giant stone ship of the Fens, lay at anchor on its low ridge above the richest, flattest lands in England, and by chance I was there when it happened.

I had gone to East Anglia to write a travel feature about the lure of this weird bit of Britain. Crowmere, Denver Sluice, Froghall Farm – its place names drip off the map like damp. Water still oozes from every Fenland pore, seeping into dikes and field drains that create endless perspectives with their precise geometry. Drive across it and always it is comparisons with the sea that spring to mind. Even the Fenland towns have the feel of seaports, close-knit havens turned in upon themselves as if unable to face the aching emptiness of the world outside.

From Quanea Drove, just outside Ely, I had watched the storm blow in from the west.

For a moment, the sun broke through the scudding cloud. Its bleak light washed over the cathedral's Gothic tower, picking out Alan of Walsingham's glorious medieval octagon against a sky as black as Fenland peat.

All day the wind howled across East Anglia, smashing fences, ripping off roofs; but Ely Cathedral stood firm, as it had done so many times before in its thousand years of history. But this storm was different. It was the forerunner of a series of freak hurricanes that strayed from their normal path and tracked south, causing havoc in Britain and other parts of Europe.

Scientists believed these rogue winds were the result of global warming and have since been proved right beyond all doubt, with serious implications for low-lying areas such as Cambridgeshire.

****

Little did I know that a storm of a totally different kind was brewing back at Fortress Wapping. After the turbulence of the struggle with the print unions it appeared that Rupert Murdoch's expanding media empire had financially overstretched itself. The *Sunday Times* would have to slim down, and an offer went out to its journalists that anyone wishing to leave could do so with the equivalent of two years' salary in their pocket.

Much as I had enjoyed my time there, the paper was no longer the same as it was in Harry Evans' glory years. I would miss my colleagues, especially Richard Girling, Philip Clarke, and Christine Walker, who had become the paper's finest travel editor, all of whom had been so supportive over the years. But my mind was made up. Fortress Wapping would see me no more, and with one bound I was over the razor wire to freedom.

Henceforth I would work from home in Dorset as a freelance travel writer. Christine Walker had promised that I could still write for her, but at the same time I was now free to write for others, including the *Daily Telegraph*, where Michael Kerr, a former colleague, was now their deputy travel editor.

Two assignments stood out that year. One was to East Berlin in February, where East Germany was stirring in the unfamiliar warmth of a new political climate after its 40-year winter.

The queue at Checkpoint Charlie moved quickly. Germany's most famous cold-war frontier post had been robbed of its former spy-thriller image, yet its seedy atmosphere still managed to provide an odd frisson as I crossed into the East.

Half an hour later I was watching the *Mauerspechte* (wall-peckers), souvenir-hunters dismantling the Berlin Wall with hammer and chisel. The sound of their tapping echoed beneath the Brandenburg Gate and across the empty space of what, until the previous November, had been a deadly no man's land.

The sightseers were in a festive mood. There was a heady sense of living in momentous times, the Wall, that monstrous schism between the two great power blocs, had been reduced to a linear billboard of graffiti. Now, everywhere, the black, red and gold of West Germany was being flaunted from street windows.

Soon I was heading south across the floodplains of the Elbe, speeding down the autobahns of the Third Reich into a lurid photo-chemical sunset thrown up by the factory chimneys of the Bitterfeld, an apt name for one of the most polluted towns in Europe.

Atmospheric pollution in the German Democratic Republic was a fact of life. It emanated not only from the factories but also from the poisonous exhausts of old jalopies – Wartburgs and Trabants, the only cars most East Germans could buy. Above all it came from burning brown lignite coal, one of the country's few abundant natural resources, which painted the air with sepia tones and gave every town and city an acrid bronchial reek reminiscent of the old London smog of my childhood.

In Erfurt I took a tram through its cobbled streets to eat at the 14th-century Gildehaus restaurant in the Fischmarkt. The place was packed, mostly with West Germans who had never been in the East before. Strangers in their own land, they were there on a free-spending voyage of discovery. 'It's so cheap for us,' said one, calling for a third bottle of wine between mouthfuls of black cherries and ice cream. 'Eating out costs so little we're finding it hard to get through all our money'.

Next day, following the tortuous back roads from village to village, I found myself in the Thüringer Wald, a rolling range of pine-clad ridges, the highest a shade under a thousand metres. In winter there was cross-country skiing here, and in summer, East Germans flocked to the woods to follow its rustic paths on foot. Some tracks ran for miles beside tumbling streams. Others climbed through aisles of beech, heading for the high ground where the tall pines grow, closing ranks in dim perspectives that shut out the sky and fill the world with a resinous silence.

To explore the eternal twilight of the Thüringer Wald is to peer deep into the German psyche. No other people in Europe love their dense forests with such pagan fervour. In these wolfish woods, thick with hobgoblin shadows and mushroomy smells, you might still catch an echo of the Brothers Grimm. But in the end, I found their black magic oppressive and was glad to be back in more open country around Arnstadt.

Pines still bristled along the hog-backed ridges, but in between lay a far-reaching countryside of hedge-less fields, with sometimes a lonely watchtower where hunters waited for the deer to come down from the woods at dusk. Plum trees grew beside the roads, and in between the woods you could see a long way, making it easy to imagine the glitter of distant armies wheeling on the sunlit plains. Church towers, each with a spire like a Kaiser's helmet, rose from every fold and hollow, where half-timbered farmhouses slept under steep red roofs in a nest of orchards, surrounded by duck ponds, dunghills, free-range fowls and all the other rural stage props long since banished from the British countryside.

Much of East Germany, even its most historic cities, seemed frozen in a 1950s time warp. But among the uncharted villages of Thuringia, I felt I had stumbled upon an older, Arcadian past contemporary with Constable's England, which had somehow survived two world wars and 40 years of Communism.

'You know, in olden times Thuringia was known as the green heart of Germany,' said Artur Volker, the former burgomaster of Neuroda. Then aged 76, he was still living with his wife in the half-timbered farmhouse they first moved into when they married the year after I was born. They still worked with heavy horses until the farms were collectivised in 1958, but now their balconied farmhouse was silent. A wind blew through the village, shaking the Thuringian slate wall tiles with a skeletal rattle. 'You can't imagine how terrible it was to lose your land,' said Volker. 'We were supposed to give it up willingly, but it was more like a prison sentence.'

Everywhere, local people seemed pleased to see me. In Branchewinda the lady who ran the village shop told me I was the first Englishman she had ever met. Proudly she unlocked the church to show me the treasured icon above the altar. The church clock still worked, its cracked bell sending a cloud of sparrows flying into the churchyard beech.

Beneath the tree was a memorial to the German dead of two world wars: 28 men from a village of fewer than 150 souls. Greiner, Katzenmaier, Pohl, Stuberach, I read their names while skylarks sang in the open fields and the churchyard crocuses turned their faces to the sun.

How and where had they died, I wondered. Could one of them have been a member of the bomber crew who brought the ceiling down on my head when I was growing up in the Blitz? Or the mortally wounded Messerschmidt pilot I had seen slumped in his burning cockpit above the rooftops of Briarwood Road? Somehow, the intervening decades had washed away the anger and deep hostility of the 1940s, and here in Germany's rural heartland, in a countryside that mirrored my own in so many ways, I felt only a sense of sadness and reconciliation.

****

My other outstanding travel assignment of 1990 could hardly have been more different, taking me 16,000 miles south to Namibia. David Coulson was the son of a diplomat, who grew up in England but had been living in Nairobi, where he won international acclaim as a photographer and would later become the co-founder and chairman of the Trust for African Rock Art (TARA).

Over the years we had worked on several assignments in Kenya and Botswana, but I had never been to Namibia, the country he knew best and which he now planned to show me from end to end in the beaten-up old Toyota Land Cruiser he kept in Windhoek.

There was no road to Purros. Only the ruts of old tyre tracks disappearing into the mountains and deserts of Kaokoland. Purros itself was nothing but a scattering of shacks and mud huts belonging to the Himba, pastoralists who dress in skins and roam the ochre hills with their goats and cattle.

As we lurched down the dried-up bed of the Gomatum River, a tributary of the Hoarusib, the sky turned black and thunder rumbled in the hills. 'Is it going to rain?' I asked. David shook his head. 'Not in the desert,' he said. But even as he spoke, the first fat spots began to fall. Moments later we were in the thick of a ferocious tropical storm – and it was precisely then that fate decided we should have a puncture.

There was nothing for it but to leap out into the lashing rain and change the wheel. In seconds we were soaked to the skin. When at last the wheel was fixed, I took off my desert boots and poured the water out. What an odd way, I thought, to begin one of the hottest weeks of my life in one of the driest places on earth.

Namibia is the last great wilderness in southern Africa. Imagine a country four times the size of Britain with fewer than 1.2 million people at that time. Much of the land is desert. Some of its rivers do not run for years. In some places no rain has fallen for close on a century, and to explore such inhospitable terrain requires local expertise. That was why we were driving to Purros, to meet Louw and Amy Schoeman who were going to take us to the Skeleton Coast.

The Skeleton Coast National Park is a strip of desert up to 40 kilometres wide, running for some 500 kilometres from the Kunene River on the Angolan border down to the Ugab River near Cape Cross. When the park was proclaimed in 1971, the northern sector was set aside as a wilderness area in which only limited tourism would be allowed. In 1977 it was Louw Schoeman, a lawyer and one-time diamond prospector and tour operator who was awarded the concession to operate fly-in safaris there. 'Never underestimate the desert,' he said. 'It isn't hostile, but it can be dangerous – even deadly if you don't know it. But I have been coming here for 30 years and it is just like moving around in my own living room. I love it. In my opinion it's one of the most beautiful places on earth.'

From Purros we followed Schoeman across country, traversing immense gravel plains with no sign of life except for a few springboks and ostriches on the furthest horizons until we came at sunset to his camp on the Khumib River. The river had flowed a month earlier after heavy rains upcountry, but now it was bone dry again.

When I went to bed, I was sure I could smell the sea on the night breeze, although the coast was a good 12 kilometres away, and when I awoke, I could hear the roar of the Atlantic surf.

'We're paranoid about vehicle tracks up here,' said Louw as we set out through the dune fields towards the sea. 'The desert is easy to scar and slow to heal. I can show you tracks made in 1943 to rescue survivors from the wreck of the *Dunedin Star*. They look as if they were made only last week.'

The secret of driving in dune fields, I discovered, is to deflate the tyres until they are like squashy balloons. Then, with the vehicle in four-wheel drive, you put your foot down and float through the soft sand with a sensation akin to skiing in powder snow; and as we sailed up over the final crest there was the glorious sight of green and white Atlantic rollers crashing on an empty shore.

Up and down the coast as far as the eye could see, the sands were littered with the flotsam of centuries: a tangle of ships' masts, planks and spars, with here and there the bleached skeleton of a great whale, killed by the American whaling fleets a hundred years ago. Kelp gulls watched us at a distance, and ghost crabs danced away through the wind-blown spume, but ours were the only footprints.

Beside the Atlantic I felt oddly at ease. Alone with my thoughts I sat on the beach as a fog bank came rolling in, heavy with the smell of kelp. The damp sea mist clung to my bare legs, but I was not cold. I walked for miles, relieved to be out of the desert heat, listening to the gulls, beachcombing for agate pebbles among the jackal prints and sea-urchin shells. There was never a day when I was not happy in Africa, but the sound of the surf suddenly triggered a wave of nostalgia for Chesil Beach and the green hills of Dorset, and for once, for a moment, I wished I was back home.

Next day we flew over the Skeleton Coast on our way north to Kunene, where Schoeman had another camp, looking across the river into Angola. We flew low over a colony of Cape fur seals and narrowly missed a flock of Damara terns, which rose from the water in front of us. Had we hit them they would have had the effect of a ground-to-air missile, and I began to understand how he had acquired his nickname: 'Low-Flying Schoeman'.

At last, we came to the mouth of the Kunene River and followed it inland across a scene of utter desolation. To the south lay nothing but salt pans, a terrifying emptiness reaching away into the dunes and mountain ranges of Kaokoland. To the north rose the sun-scorched rocks of Angola. 'Amazing to think that most of this country has never had a human foot on it,' Schoeman yelled above the engine's roar. 'Not even a bushman.'

It seemed impossible that there could be any safe place to land in this burnt and broken country, but eventually a strip appeared on a wide plain and we stepped out into the gasping heat of late afternoon. A vehicle was waiting to take us to Louw's camp. The recent rains had raised a brief flush of grass from the red sand, but already it was withering in the heat. To the south a range of nameless hills raised their granite heads. Rock kestrels whistled among the crags and larks flew up as we drove along the stony ridges.

By the time we reached camp the sun was setting. Shadows seeped out of the ground like smoke, filling the hollows of the hills above the gorge in which the river hissed and swirled in flood. There was a tiny swimming pool among the rocks (the river itself was full of crocodiles) and what bliss it was to cool off and then sit with a cold beer and watch the lightning flickering in the Angolan mountains. 'You don't come here to see animals,' said Schoeman. 'You come for the remoteness, the ruggedness. Mass tourism has no place here, but a few people will pay for the privilege of coming to such a wild area.'

We left Kunene after breakfast to fly back to the Khumib. Once more that savage landscape unfolded beneath our wings, the sands a smouldering Martian red, the soda pans blinding, the mountains flayed by wind and sun. I was glad to have seen the Kunene, but relieved to escape from its brooding hostility.

At the Khumib we made our farewells to the Schoemans and set off south down the Skeleton Coast. After an hour or so we came to the mouth of the Hoarusib. There had been more storms inland and the river was running. We waded across to see if it was too deep to drive. The water was flowing strongly and rising as we watched, swirling downstream in sudden surges that spread out across the sand. It was now or never. Slowly we nosed into the flood and drove across it obliquely with the water lapping at the doors.

Down on the shore, bathed in the golden Atlantic light, springboks were feeding. It seemed incongruous to find them beside the sea, but sometimes, said Coulson, desert-dwelling elephants followed the sand rivers down to the coast, leaving their giant footprints on the beach. And from time to time a desert lion would come wandering out of Damaraland to scavenge for seal carcasses in the surf.

Our destination was Mowe Bay, where the national park rangers were based. With its bleached driftwood shacks and small gardens heaped with fishing nets, whalebones, elephant skulls and other flotsam, the bleak little settlement resembled the setting for a Steinbeck novel. Yet despite its remoteness it seemed to attract a succession of the most remarkable and gifted people.

One of the shacks was the home of Des and Jen Bartlett, who had lived and worked in the Namibian parks for 14 years. Over a breakfast of tea and kippers they explained how they had been using microlight aircraft to shoot the first film of desert-dwelling elephants migrating through the dunes.

Later, after a brief sojourn in Swakopmund we set off again, this time into the true Namib – 'the place where there is nothing' – a sun-struck wilderness of gravel plains above which mirages of distant mountain tops appeared as rocky islands in a trembling sea of blue. High rolling dunes marched south with us down to the western horizon, like the Sussex Downs painted red, until we camped at a place called Homeb.

In late afternoon we crossed the riverbed and climbed up out of the valley to watch the sun descend behind the dunes. We came to a stony plateau where sandblasted pebbles of clear white and yellow crystal glittered in the sand like fallen stars. (I still have one beside my desk as I write. When I found it, I wondered if it might be a diamond. Alas, it is only quartz, but a precious memento all the same.)

Nothing grew here save a few sparse grey tufts of grass that creaked and hissed in the wind – yet scatterings of old, dry spoor showed that gemsboks and zebras had passed this way. Back in camp, night came swiftly. A full moon rose, and in the clear air every detail of its cratered surface was visible through my binoculars. We barbecued the steaks we had bought in Swakopmund and ate them with potatoes and onions wrapped in foil and baked in the embers, washed down with beers from the cool box.

Afterwards, stretched out in my sleeping bag, I lay on my back and looked up at the brightest stars in Africa. From faraway downriver came the sepulchral hoot of an owl and the faint cries of jackals keening in the dunes; then nothing more.

Above Homeb the course of the river cuts through a range of cindery hills into the desolate Huasib canyonlands. This is where two Germans, Hermann Korn and Henno Martin, with their dog Otto, hid for nearly three years to avoid internment by the South Africans during the Second World War. Henno told their story in a book, *The Sheltering Desert*, in which he graphically described their solitary lives, shooting game and searching for water in the bottom of the canyons.

Distance lends these far-reaching, barren lands the surreal perspective of a painting by Salvador Dali, with the unearthly shark's-fin shapes of mountain ranges thrusting over the horizon. Here, in the pitiless heat of the Namib, the earth's rocks are being tested to destruction, blowtorched by the sun, sandblasted by the searing winds and broken down into fissured gullies and ravines in which the eye cries out for a green tree or a pool of water.

All my life I have loved wilderness and wild places, but the Namib's unrelenting hostility defeated me. In its furnace heat I found my spirit wilting like a dying flower. Only in the last golden hour before sunset, and again in the first cool hour of dawn, did the desert relent, allowing deep shadows to soften its harsh contours, transforming it into a silent world of unearthly beauty.

Before returning to England at the end of the safari, a pilot friend of David Coulson volunteered to take us for one last look at the Skeleton Coast. We flew low, following its lonely shores south past Sandwich Bay, where colonies of Cape fur seals lay in dense brown packs, staring at the jackals that preyed on the sick and the dead.

Further south again we flew over the wreck of the *Eagle*, a 19th-century barque with her ribs and spars sticking out of the sand. We made a low pass along the beach, the green waves breaking beneath our wheels, then rose until I could see the endless emptiness of the coast reaching all the way to where the Orange River lay over the horizon.

By the time we turned for home the flowing summits of the dunes had already begun to glow in the evening light. From the air the Namib and its giant dunes appeared as lifeless as the moon; but then came a sight to lift the heart, as out of the shadows a group of gemsboks came galloping, their horns held high like lances, hoofs kicking up puffs of sand as they pounded up the smooth incline and cantered away into the setting sun.

CHAPTER TWENTY-ONE

IN April 1992 I returned to Dorset after an idyllic week in the Yorkshire Dales. Normally, when I took the train home from London Waterloo to Dorchester, Sarah would be waiting to drive me back home; but this time there was no sign of her, or our little red Volkswagen Golf. Instead, I was greeted by a taxi driver, who explained that he had been requested to pick me up and take me to Powerstock.

What had happened, I wondered. Perhaps the car had broken down. I was not unduly worried, but when I got home it was parked outside in its usual spot. The kitchen door was unlocked, and the Rayburn was alight, giving out a good heat, but the cottage was empty. Even Lopez, our elderly tabby cat, had vanished. Then I saw the note lying on the kitchen table, handwritten in biro on a single sheet of paper. There was no acknowledgement as to whom it was addressed. 'This may come as a surprise to you,' it began, 'but I have left you.' Then followed a warning not to go looking for her, and an explanation for taking the cat but leaving everything else except a few photographs.

After the initial shock had worn off, I realised what had happened. Several times in the past she had threatened to leave. This time she had done it, although knowing who she was with and where she had gone came as no surprise at all.

There have been times in my life when I have been content to drift, happy to go with the flow; but I have always been aware enough to seize whatever opportunities came my way. Now was such a moment. I picked up the phone and called Annabelle to explain what had happened. Then I paused, drew a deep breath, and said: 'Well, that's how it is. So, will you marry me?'

I knew the answer before I heard it, but it was still reassuring to have my proposal accepted. I packed some clothes, picked up my passport and binoculars, locked up the cottage and set off for East Anglia.

****

For the next nine months I became the youngest resident at Forncett Manor, the care home Annabelle ran in Norfolk. We lived together in the converted coach house adjoining the main house, which had once been a suffragan bishop's palace, sharing our home with two Labradors and an elderly tomcat called Grey Job.

The Manor stood set back from the road in three acres of rose beds and manicured lawns overlooking an ornamental fish pond and a mighty copper beech which had lost its crown in the great storm of 1987 when winds gusting up to a hundred miles an hour had ravaged much of southern England, killing 18 people and uprooting 15 million trees.

A paddock ran the length of the grounds in which Annabelle kept her horse, a cob named Fudge, and his inseparable companion, a donkey called Comfy. At one end, protected from the wind by a handsome brick crinkle-crankle wall, stood a pen where a dozen hens were kept, and at the other was a vegetable patch where

Charlie, the octogenarian gardener, grew everything from lettuces to potatoes and tomatoes for Annabelle's 17 frail and elderly residents, including her mother in the final stages of Alzheimer's.

Looking after them was a full-time job for Annabelle and her staff of 22, all of whom became good friends of mine and welcomed my unexpected entry into their lives. As for me, it was an insight into a world I had never seen before, and I was humbled by the way in which all the residents, no matter what little peccadillos they might have had, were loved and cared for with such kindness and compassion that at times I was moved close to tears.

In Annabelle's spare moments we walked the Labradors on the marsh, an expanse of rough pasture with a stream running through it, where green sandpipers flew up with liquid cries. At other times we went cycling down empty lanes that wound among the vast flat fields of Norfolk or drove into Norwich on shopping expeditions; and of course, Annabelle was eager to show me Aldeburgh, where she had grown up, an hour away on the Suffolk coast.

Apart from the time I had first met Annabelle, Suffolk was new to me. Everything, from the lie of the land to the picture-book villages with their pastel-coloured cottages and pantile rooftops, was so different to Dorset; but slowly I came to love it, although it would never replace the West Country in my affections.

I particularly liked Aldeburgh, an old-fashioned seaside town with one eye looking over its shoulder to where the lower reaches of the Alde estuary made their way down to the coast. Back then it still seemed trapped in a 1930s time warp, a gentle backwater on the way to nowhere, marooned on East Anglia's broad backside.

In Tudor times its timbered Moot Hall marked the town centre; but everything to the east of it has been swallowed up by the advancing sea, like drowned Dunwich, higher up the coast beyond Southwold. The days when fleets of smacks would sail from Aldeburgh every summer to fish for cod in Icelandic waters were gone for ever; but longshoremen in yellow oilskins still winched their boats up the shelving shingle beach and stored their gear in tarred wooden huts across the road from the Wentworth Hotel.

I was sorry never to have met Annabelle's father, who by all accounts was quite a character, and even sadder that my parents would never meet Annabelle, who they would have adored. My mother had died in December 1981 and my father lived on for eight lonely years until he, too, died in Epsom Hospital. Apart from my two brothers, my cousin Peter now living in New Jersey, my Aunt Vi and her daughter Jennifer, the family I had grown up with had all gone.

Now, suddenly, I had become part of a new family and it was profoundly gratifying to be so warmly welcomed by Annabelle's siblings. Marlies, the eldest of her three sisters, was married to Christopher Barnett, a circuit judge who had fought the Mau Mau in Kenya and become a district commissioner before returning to England.

Alyson, three years younger than Marlies, was married to Bill Sylvester and lived in Rickmansworth, where he was deeply involved in the local amateur dramatic scene.

The youngest was Sarah, known to all as Poohdie, who had severe learning difficulties and lived in a care home in Norwich.

As for her brother Michael, since taking over the running of the Wentworth from his father he had transformed it into one of the county's finest hotels, and lived with Emma, his partner at Flash Corner, an idyllic half-timbered cottage in sight of Minsmere, the RSPB's flagship reserve.

Of all the places I got to know in East Anglia, Minsmere stood out above the rest.

For decades it has been the pride of British bird reserves. This was where the avocet returned to breed after an absence of well over a century, and where more than half of our marsh harriers are born. Leased to the RSPB by a sympathetic landowner in 1948, the reserve was later purchased for £250,000, a daunting sum in those days; but in conservation terms Minsmere is beyond price.

Within its 1,500 acres is a range of habitats few other reserves can match: a rich mosaic of meres and reed beds, dunes, heath and swarthy woods all bounded by a shingle shore. Its strategic position on the Suffolk coast provides a safe landfall for regular migrants as well as unsuspected continental vagrants such as spoonbills and purple herons. But above all, at a time when wetlands are everywhere under threat, Minsmere's enclaves have become a permanent refuge for a host of species, from otters to bitterns.

In early spring and summer, marsh harriers beat over the reeds on mothlike wings, and at dusk the strange churring calls of nightjars carry across the sleeping heath. But winter brings its own rewards and was the time I loved the best, when Bewick's swans with buttercup bills flew in from Arctic Russia and the reserve sank back into its older, more elemental guise. Alone under the low grey skies, among the impenetrable reeds and the chain-mail glitter of the mere, the centuries fall away and Minsmere becomes a Dark Ages fen lifted straight from the pages of *Beowulf.*

Here I would sit in one of the RSPB's wooden hides, sipping hot soup and watching snipe probing the marsh for invertebrates. Outside, there was no sound but the venomous hiss of the wind in the reeds; while inland, above the surge of woods, forlorn in the midwinter light, grey geese were flying.

Once much of East Anglia was like this; just reeds and birds and empty coast, shingle scrunching underfoot and the scream of gulls on the North Sea wind. Now Minsmere is one of the last wild places where marshland birds can breed in safety. Yet even here, like a symbol of the unknown future waiting at Minsmere's gates, a concrete monolith frowns across the marsh: the uncompromising silhouette of Sizewell's nuclear power station complex.

****

In the weeks that followed I got to know every inch of Minsmere, but at the same time, amidst all the turmoil of moving to Suffolk, I had also been talking to my lawyer about Sarah's departure. The result, impossible to have imagined only months ago, was that I would be divorced and remarried within a year.

The wedding took place in January 1993 in Aldeburgh's parish church. The winter light streamed through John Piper's stained-glass windows, a memorial tribute to Benjamin Britten, shining down on a packed congregation that included my daughter as Annabelle processed towards me on her brother's arm while I stood at the altar with my best man, Dick Girling.

After the reception at the Wentworth Hotel, we spent our honeymoon in Kenya and it was wonderful to watch Annabelle's reactions as she fell under the spell of Africa's wildlife and wild places just as I had done so many years earlier. She told me later that, during the early stages of our courtship, she had confided to her sisters that there was someone new in her life, a travel writer who went regularly to Africa. 'Go for it,' they urged her. 'Who knows – you might even get to see the world.'

Now here she was, watching lions in the Masai Mara where Ari Grammaticus, the owner of Governor's Camp, had generously given us a balloon safari as a wedding present. We also spent a few idyllic days on Mfangano Island in the middle of Lake Victoria before ending up with a week beside the Indian Ocean in Malindi at Kingfisher Lodge.

The lodge belonged to Herbie Paul, one of the best big game fishermen on the Kenyan coast. I had met him on an earlier trip to Tsavo, where he owned a small safari camp on the Galana River. Born in Rostock, Germany, he had come to Kenya when he was only six months old and was now the president of the Malindi Sea Fishing Club.

Hemingway had fished at Malindi in 1954 and, given another 10 years, Herbie might easily have passed as the unforgettable marlin fisherman described in the opening page of *The Old Man and the Sea*: 'Everything about him was old except his eyes.'

In 1986, with Angus, his son, on board their boat, *Tina*, they once caught 16 sailfish in a single morning.

I, too, had gone fishing with Herbie and caught a sailfish, a creature of spectacular beauty, all violet and shining silver, with peacock-blue spots on its great dorsal fin as it leapt for its life at the end of my line.

Afterwards, staring at its leathery corpse in the scuppers, its quicksilver colours turned to leather, I was overcome with remorse. I knew Annabelle would have hated it. Not so much a triumph as an act of murder; so rather than put to sea we simply lazed around by Herbie's pool, soaking up the sun and eating lobsters for supper until it was time to fly back to East Anglia.

****

I enjoyed my unexpected Suffolk sojourn. How could it have been otherwise, living with the woman I loved? But all the time I was secretly pining for the green hills of home. The West Country was deep in my DNA and I longed for the day when I might return. Annabelle also dreamed of a future in Dorset, but that meant selling Forncett Manor, an impossibility so long as her mother was still living there.

Then, as so often happens, the decision was taken out of our hands. Her mother's health took a turn for the worse, and one cloudless evening that summer, with Annabelle and I both at her bedside, just at that moment when the last of the light was beginning to fade, her soul flew out into the oncoming darkness.

In the months that followed, Annabelle found a buyer. For one last time we walked over the marsh, then made our tearful farewells with the staff, packed Grey Job and the two Labradors into Annabelle's car and set off for Dorset.

CHAPTER
TWENTY-TWO

SAFELY back home again in Powerstock, I started looking for somewhere else to live. I had always been happy there, even though the cottage was small and the garden even smaller; but Annabelle wanted us to make a clean break with the past and make a new home, especially as there were now two dogs and a cat to look after. I agreed, albeit reluctantly. It was not the cottage itself I would miss but its location. Over the years I had grown used to living in the shadow of Eggardon and the thought of having to move elsewhere was hard to bear.

The previous year, while living in Suffolk, Annabelle and I had driven down to Dorset now and again just to keep an eye on the cottage, which was now lying empty. On one such visit we arrived to find all the gardens in the parish open to visitors to raise money for the church.

In West Milton, a mile down the road from Powerstock, we bumped into Andrew Lobb, a staunch friend who had acted as my solicitor when I bought Way Cottage. He was standing outside Spick Hatch, a long Hamstone house with its back to the road and a garden that fell away into the valley below. I had driven past countless times on my way to and from Bridport, but had never been inside, even though I knew its owners.

Andrew offered to take us around and we followed him through the gate in the wall into a garden dominated by an ancient pear tree.

Beyond lay a gravel path dropping down past a water garden to an orchard where apple trees grew beside a stream, and with every step we gasped with delight at the changing vista. On the other side of the stream, the land rose steeply, creating a skyline of sensuously rounded hills, and from somewhere came the sound of water spilling over a weir.

Annabelle turned to me and whispered in my ear. 'Are you thinking what I'm thinking?' I understood exactly what she meant, because right then I knew this was where I wanted to live. It even had a couple of meadows and a stable where Annabelle could keep her horse and donkey.

On the way back we met the owners, Major-General Reynell Taylor, a former commander of the British Forces in Cyprus, and Rosemary, his wife. I complimented them on their garden and told them we were in the process of looking for somewhere else to live. 'In the unlikely event you should ever want to sell Spick Hatch,' I said, half-joking, 'do let us know.'

To our amazement, Rosemary said they were indeed planning to move to Taunton, where they hoped to send their young son to school. We begged her to give us first refusal and drove back to Powerstock to put the cottage up for sale.

****

Since my return to Dorset, all my local friends had been curious to see my new bride, and a succession of dinner parties followed. I also wanted to take Annabelle on my favourite walks around the parish to show her what a special corner of England she had chosen to live in, and how easy it was to visit Cornwall from here. I was surprised to discover she had never been and could not wait to take her across the Tamar to introduce her to a dear friend.

Dick Treleaven was a man as Cornish as his name. In his time, he had been an infantry commander, a painter and falconer; but ever since I had known him, he had spent most of his life watching peregrines on the cliffs between Bude and Port Isaac. 'They are an obsession with me,' he confessed, an understatement if ever there was one.

His passion for these glorious raptors had begun in London in the late 1940s. He had just returned from fighting the Japanese in the Burma campaign during the Second World War and was window-shopping in Piccadilly when a painting caught his eye. It was a portrait of a Greenland falcon by George Lodge, perhaps the finest wildlife painter of his day.

He went inside and saw more pictures, including a peregrine that captured his imagination. 'Two things happened as a result,' he explained. 'I began to paint, and I returned home determined to see a wild peregrine and discovered to my surprise that Cornwall was the best place in England for observing them.'

With his arms waving like a conductor at the last night of the Proms and his eyes ablaze with a wild predatory gleam, I still remember him describing the first kill he ever saw – a hunt that ended when the tiercel (male peregrine) grabbed a pigeon directly above him. 'Feathers trickled down over my head and shoulders,' he said. 'I felt as if I had been anointed.'

In 1951 he took up falconry, the better to be able to paint hawks, joining the close-knit and eccentric brotherhood that met regularly at Hallworthy to fly their birds on Bodmin Moor. His first bird was a goshawk called Crasher that he used to carry around Bude on his fist. 'One day I heard these two kids talking as I went past,' he told me. 'There he goes,' said one to the other, 'old Plus-Fours and his bloody sparrow.'

Crasher was followed by a succession of other hawks, including a lanner falcon from Benghazi and another goshawk called Sammy Snatchit who escaped and was last seen perched on a railway signal in Basingstoke. But he never kept a peregrine. 'They owe allegiance to nobody,' he declared. 'I know the peregrine is the falconer's dream, but I could never own one. It is too noble a bird to be captive. It must be free. It belongs high on a clifftop, and that is where I like to see it fly and hear it scream.'

When I first knew him his wife, Marge, was still alive. He had never learned to drive, and so it was Marge who took him from Launceston to the cliffs and back. Then Marge had died, leaving him rudderless and inconsolable, dependent on friends and fellow peregrine fanatics to drive him to the coast.

When I introduced Annabelle to Dick, I knew straight away they would like each other. Because she came from Suffolk, he called her Boadicea, after the warrior queen of the Iceni whose Iron Age realm lay not far from Aldeburgh, and thus began a friendship that would last until he died in 2009.

With Annabelle at the wheel, we drove down to the coast along a narrow lane between squat hedge banks of Delabole slate, built Cornish style in herringbone patterns from whose crevices the fleshy leaves of pennywort erupted like green blisters.

The day was cheerless, but the coast was alive with birds. Herring gulls hung in the updraughts, crook-winged, wailing as they rose and fell about the pillars and buttresses of yawning chasms. Somewhere a raven grunted beneath an overhang.

Fulmars gabbled as they planed over the swell and boomeranged around the cove before landing on guano-spattered crags, and above the mumble of the sea arose the fretful piping of oystercatchers and the deeper, menacing bark of a black-backed gull.

The wind was raw, and we cast around the lichen-scabbed rocks for a place to shelter and scan the black cliff on the far side of the cove, looking for the resident pair of peregrines whose eyrie was hidden at the back of a grassy ledge halfway up the rock face.

Even before we found them, I could hear them screaming, and suddenly there they were, both birds together, flickering in from the sea. Almost at once the female (known simply as the falcon) disappeared behind the headland, but I watched the tiercel land on a cushion of thrift and begin to tug at something anchored firmly beneath his yellow feet. Grey feathers floated away on the wind and I knew we had just missed a kill.

On another part of the cliff a pair of ravens had lodged their nest of sticks in a narrow rock chimney. Their breeding season had begun even before that of the peregrines. For weeks, the female had been sitting on a clutch of sea-green eggs. Now, although there were chicks in the nest, both parents spent more time in the air, tumbling and flying in perfect unison, wing tip to wing tip, feet dangling. Sometimes one bird would peel away in a long, looping dive, only to join its mate moments later, their black pinions almost touching, like outstretched fingers.

It was now nearly noon, time for lunch. I dug into my backpack, unwrapped some pasties and poured coffee into plastic mugs we held with both hands to thaw our frozen fingers. At that moment, just as I was about to raise the mug to my lips there was a sudden commotion and every gull and jackdaw on the cliff was aloft, wheeling and crying.

It did not take long to find out the reason why. Halfway down the cliff the two ravens had cornered a buzzard on a ledge near their nest. The buzzard was clearly unhappy and mewed plaintively as it sought to defend itself; but the ravens were merciless. Their throats swelled, their hackles rose, and their guttural barks rang around the cove as they chased the buzzard from ledge to ledge.

At times it seemed as if they were deliberately baiting their victim. While one raven shuffled forward, croaking loudly, its mate would sneak up behind and tweak the buzzard by the tail. Once they almost forced it into the sea; but eventually it managed to gain height and flap ignominiously to safety, mobbed by gulls until finally it took refuge in a hedge. Meanwhile the ravens, having tired of their sport, were performing a victory roll over the cliffs. High overhead twirled the bold buccaneers. Their jet-black plumage shone with glossy green and purple glints as they turned in a single shaft of sunlight and disappeared beyond the headland.

So intent were we on watching them that we never saw the falcon return to her favourite hunting perch. One minute there was nothing but bare rock; the next she was sitting there, a furious gargoyle, glaring out to sea.

Her sudden appearance was typical of peregrines. How swift they are, how mysterious their secret comings and goings; assured and complete, they belong to a world more ancient than our own, moved by visions we can only guess at, living a freedom we can never know.

By now the sun had broken through, although the sea wind was as cold as ever, and both the falcon and the tiercel were aloft. Even through my binoculars they were mere specks, yet they seemed to dominate the landscape beneath. At first it appeared they were simply revelling in the joy of flight, carving immense parabolas across the sky, and almost playing with the pigeons that scattered in panic at every leisurely stoop. And still we waited.

Afternoon came. The wind dropped. The sun became warmer and a big, mottled seal appeared at the base of the cliffs, bobbing like a bottle in the cove's green depths.

Winter or summer, the magic of this savage coast never fails. On either side the cliffs fall sheer, sometimes breaking away to form barnacled reefs and towers of bristling rock at whose feet the heaving swell booms and subsides with sinister gasps.

Above us the falcon was back at her pitch. She had evolved a method of hunting that is entirely suited to the lie of the land and the predictable movements of the pigeons that were her favourite prey. When she left the cliff, she flew like a fugitive, dropping swiftly towards the sea to disappear behind the headland. There she would let the updraught lift her, riding with it until she was in view once more.

Inland, gulls were circling in a thermal and she glided towards them, ringing up on the warm currents of air until she was no more than a black star blinking among the crests and summits of the towering clouds. Now she drifted, going towards the sun, following the line of the coast for perhaps a mile, to the inlet where the pigeons breed. She had learned the ways of pigeons, which leave the cliffs every day and pass up the shallow valley to feed in the fields.

From her lofty ambush among the clouds, nothing escaped her binocular vision: white specks of gulls glancing over the plough-land; black rooks and grapeshot bursts of starlings; but what she was looking for was the piebald flicker of feral pigeons and at once she accelerated. Her bow-bent wings beat faster, so fast that I could almost sense the hunger burning inside her, driving her forward with an unmistakable sense of purpose.

Unable to take my eyes off her in case I lost her, I could not yet see what she could see, but knew that she was hunting, and I remembered something Dick once told me: 'Peregrines don't really *chase* pigeons,' he said. 'Their whole strategy is based on interception.' And he was right. Somewhere beneath her, still unaware of danger, a flock of pigeons was heading for home.

From a mile high the falcon tipped forward, folded her wings and then stooped, faster than a falling stone. Her dive carried her below the skyline, where she was harder to see against the dun colours of the moor; but now for the first time I picked up her quarry. The pigeons scattered as she swooped beneath them and then bounded up to snatch at a straggler. She missed - levelled out over Hendra, skimming over the bare fields with white gulls boiling in her wake. On she flew, streaking low over the lichen-covered hedge banks, past squat church towers and farms slate-roofed against the gales - and missed again.

But she was not done yet. Now she ringed up, turned and flew directly towards us, passing overhead in an effortless glide, her wings dark blades, yellow feet bunched up behind. I could see her round head swivelling and briefly felt her gaze upon me as she scanned the ground beneath, and as she swung out over the cliffs the sun outlined her body in a wash of burning gold. Once more she climbed between the clouds, the beautiful barbarian, 'waiting on at her pitch' in the words of the old falconers, a thousand feet above the headland.

Then she put in another searing stoop, corkscrewing down towards her target; and this time her dive took her right into the cove, whipping low over the waves as if intent on committing suicide by smashing into the cliffs; but at the last moment she bounded upwards almost vertically to alight on a buttress near the eyrie. Grey feathers drifted away from the motionless shadow beneath her feet and her triumphant scream floated back across the abyss.

I turned to Annabelle. 'What did you think of that?' Her eyes were shining, and I knew we had made another convert as we made our way back to Dick's bungalow in South Petherwin before driving home to Dorset.

CHAPTER
TWENTY-THREE

IN 1994 someone else who would become a lifelong friend entered our lives. I had first met Christopher Swann when I had sailed around Land's End aboard the *Marques*, the three-masted barque which featured on television as HMS *Beagle* in the BBC's epic series on the life of Charles Darwin. That was when she was making a round-Britain voyage organised by Richard Demarco, director of the Demarco art gallery in Edinburgh as a kind of ocean-going prelude to the Edinburgh Festival, and Swanny, as he was known to one and all, was one of the crew.

Swanny has spent most of his adult life at sea, including a stint as a diver in the Royal Navy before he left the service to go adventuring on square-riggers and later fell in love with the *Marguerite Explorer*, a 73-ton Danish trawler built in 1934. 'She was everything a sea boat should be,' he said, 'solid and reassuring, but also with a gloriously sexy curved counter stern and a delicious sweep to her deck.'

By then he had already decided to base himself in Oban, on the west coast of Scotland, offering sailing holidays in the Hebrides. Having sailed there before and read all Gavin Maxwell's books, he knew how rich the wildlife was. But when he first arrived, he had no idea that these Hebridean waters are a favourite feeding ground for dolphins and minke whales.

Later in the year the orcas would also arrive, and he remembers seeing them for the first time, eight-ton sea monsters with dorsal fins like dinghy sails. 'There were seven of them cruising off North Uist,' he told me, 'and they looked exactly like what they are, lords of the sea at the top of the food chain.'

Swanny became obsessed with them – so much so that he once followed a group of killer whales for 14 hours. Food and drink were irrelevant. The sun scorched his eyes and he found himself drawn irresistibly into their world. 'As would happen many times thereafter,' he said, 'I simply became a whale.'

Every summer he followed the whales' path, living an idyllic life beyond reach of the telephone, in a world without television or traffic fumes, and it was then he approached me to see if I would be interested in writing a travel feature about the holidays he offered on board the *Marguerite Explorer*. 'The Hebrides are an undiscovered paradise,' he wrote. 'All you have to do is jump on a train to Oban.' And that is exactly what we did.

For seven glorious midsummer days we cruised around the Minch, scampering among seal skerries and lonely islands inhabited by otters, red deer, and eagles. Evenings aboard the *Marguerite Explorer* were filled with wine and poetry, jokes and banter, and 'the troops', as he called his guests, adored him. One wrote in the visitors' book, 'I hope the boat breaks down before we reach Oban,' and I knew exactly how he felt.

The highlight of the trip came on the last day. The previous evening, we had sailed over the sea to Skye, to Loch Scavaig at the foot of the Cuillin mountains. The pilot book called Scavaig the most dramatic anchorage in Europe and it was hard to disagree.

It was as if we had come to rest in the drowned nave of an immense and roofless cathedral whose broken walls echoed to the constant hiss of falling water. Above us the Cuillins crowded in, as dark as treachery, with snow still lying in the highest corries.

We awoke in the morning to find a fine rain falling, which served only to intensify the beauty of a world painted in a hundred shades of grey. Oystercatchers piped us on our way and Atlantic seals with Roman noses stared at us with mournful eyes from rocks polished smooth by the last Ice Age.

There was no wind. All morning we motored on through an oily calm until we came to the area Swanny called Cetacean City, so frequent are the whale sightings. Naturally, it was Swanny who saw them first. 'Minke whales on the starboard bow!'

And there they were, mother and calf, surfacing at regular intervals as they fed unhurriedly no more than 30 metres from the boat.

They were the first whales Annabelle and I had ever seen but they would not be the last. Having been encouraged by the response to my story when it was published in the *Sunday Times*, Swanny swapped his Scottish oilskins for a salt-encrusted sarong in La Paz, at the southern tip of Baja California. Here he chartered a live-aboard catamaran and began to look for whales in the fabled Sea of Cortez.

Cut off from the Pacific by the Baja, a 760-mile-long peninsula of cactus-covered mountains, the Sea of Cortez resembles a giant marine oasis in the Mexican desert. and was, in Swanny's words, 'quite simply the best place in the world to watch whales.' Here, together with Mexican waves of dolphins, lived great whales in astonishing numbers – humpbacks, fin whales, sperm whales and blue whales – the biggest animals ever to grace our planet. 'You and Annabelle have just got to come,' he wrote. It was too good an offer to refuse; but first we had to sell Way Cottage and buy our dream house in West Milton.

****

Despite its southward-facing location on the edge of a valley in one of West Dorset's most sought-after villages, the cottage was proving strangely difficult to sell. Our situation was not helped by the property market crash of the early 1990s, when house prices fell by 20 per cent. Since the Taylors had placed an eye-watering asking price on the sale of their home we would now have to scrape together everything we had, right down to our last rusty kopek if we wanted to buy it; and I still had to make a living as a freelance writer.

At least Annabelle was now free to accompany me on my journeys, and after falling under the spell of Africa during our honeymoon, she was as keen as I was to return; so, when an opportunity arose to visit Kenya's Meru National Park in June 1999, we jumped at the chance.

The occasion was the opening of Elsa's Kopje, a luxury safari lodge named after the eponymous lioness immortalised in Joy Adamson's bestselling novel, *Born Free*, and Meru itself was the park in which Elsa had been returned to the wild. Many of Meru's wild lions were the descendants of George Adamson's original man-made pride, and the red rock hilltop where George used to sit with his lions and his nightly sundowner of White Horse whisky was the site chosen for the new lodge.

'I searched for years to find the right spot,' said Stefano Cheli, the lodge's Italian-born owner. 'I looked all over Kenya. I even went down to the Serengeti, but this was the best.'

Among the guests who had flown in for the opening party were Richard Leakey, the charismatic former head of the Kenya Wildlife Service, Mark Jenkins, Meru's new park warden, and Virginia

McKenna, the film star who had played Joy in the movie version of *Born Free*. Virginia was the guest of honour, and after she had christened the lodge by smashing a bottle of champagne on the rocks, a campfire was lit on top of the kopje and the African night echoed to Stefano's robust rendition of 'Nessun Dorma'.

'The importance of Elsa and her story as told in *Born Free* is that it has changed for ever the way people think about lions,' said Virginia. I asked her how she felt about returning to a place with so many memories. 'Very strange at first,' she said, 'but then I felt quite wonderful quite quickly. I think it felt quite strange because there is nobody left. George and Joy and Elsa, and Bill my husband have all gone. I first came here with Joy in 1956 when I finished filming *Born Free*. Now, 34 years have passed and the only one left is me.'

The day after the party I went with Virginia and Mark Jenkins to visit Elsa's grave, a stone-paved mound beneath an acacia tree on the banks of the Usa River. Joy had placed a plaque there, inscribed in Old German, which translates as:

> *The wind, the wind, the heavenly child,*
> *Softly going over the stone,*
> *It strokes and kisses the lonesome night*
> *In which a deep secret lies bewitched.*
> Elsa – January 1956–January 1961.

On the way back, we stopped to climb Elsa's Rock, a spectacular whaleback of rust-red granite looming over the surrounding bush. 'Until I came to work on *Born Free*, I had no idea how it would change my life,' said Virginia. 'But Africa does that. It changes you for ever.'

****

In Dorset, our life together was measured by the changing seasons, each one marked by walks undertaken as regular rites of passage. Autumn was the time to venture into the oak woods of Powerstock Common to hear the unearthly grunting of fallow deer in rut. In winter we visited a valley just over the hill where snowdrops bloomed like fallen snow among the stream-side hazels; and as soon as springtime came, we went down to the sea to watch peregrines hunting over the Jurassic Coast.

Between West Bay and Lyme Regis, the cliffs are inherently unstable, forever foundering and falling away in colossal landslips, apart from one prominent sandstone prow whose bony ribs jut from the cliff face, providing perfect nesting ledges for gulls, ravens - and peregrines.

At Thorncombe, 500 feet above the sea stands a beacon where fires were lit to warn of the coming of the Spanish Armada. The views across Lyme Bay are stunning. On a clear day you can see Berry Head, some 50 miles away in Devon, and here we sat, binoculars in hand, scouring the cliffs for leftover pigeon kills and checking the peregrines' favourite hunting perches for fresh droppings.

As we watched and waited, floating up from the abyss, more insistent than the wailing gulls, louder than the shrilling jackdaws swirling above the Beacon, there would come a harsh, heckling cry that never failed to lift the hairs on the back of my neck.

Moments later we would spot the tiercel soaring past on switchblade wings, observing us with lustrous eyes eight times more powerful than our own as he made his way back to his eyrie a hundred feet below.

Even without the peregrines this is a coast of wonders. A few miles to the west loom the sinister cliffs of Black Ven where Mary Anning, a Victorian fossil hunter dressed in bonnet and long dress, unearthed the first ichthyosaur known to science.

These Mesozoic sea monsters lived 200 million years ago when the peregrine was still a dream on God's drawing board and the skies were ruled by nightmarish pterosaurs with long, toothed beaks and leathery wings.

Now the day of the flying lizards is done. Their bones are entombed in the same crumbling fossil beds as the ones in which Mary Anning dug out ammonite shells the size of car tyres, and peregrines are the new lords of the air.

****

So idyllic was our life in Dorset that it was hard to drag ourselves away, especially if it involved a long-haul flight in economy class to the other side of the world. Then along would come an invitation that was simply too good to miss.

Such a one was Mnemba, a small, privately owned atoll off the northeastern tip of Zanzibar. If you are looking for the ultimate Indian Ocean hideaway, this is the place.

Once it had nothing but a well, used by local fishermen who believed its waters were drawn from the very heart of Africa. Today it is one of the most sought-after holiday spots in the world – the crème de la coconut crème.

Getting there involved a 15-minute speedboat ride from a beach where fishermen were busily unloading the day's catch from their outriggers, and then a wet landing.

'Welcome to our swimming pool,' said our boatman as we waded ashore to be welcomed with a glass of cold tea and African honey. 'And there,' he said, pointing to the indigo shadows of submerged coral gardens, 'is our house reef.'

The sand was almost too hot to walk on, but the gift of shade was only a few steps away. There under the casuarina trees were 10 beachfront cottages with handwoven Zanzibar palm-frond floors and king-size beds as soft as sleep. There were no doors or windows, but privacy was absolute as each cottage was hidden in its own green tunnel of screw pines.

Barefoot casual is the Mnemba dress code. A *kikoi* (a colourful Swahili cotton wrap-around) is perfectly acceptable. For dinner: the morning's catch of kingfish, say, with a pineapple salsa, and a lemongrass *brulée* for dessert.

At all times, indolence rules. On our private veranda we whiled away the hours playing *bao*, the world's oldest board game, on a slab of carved ebony with seeds as counters. And every cottage has its own beach bed, primitive but supremely comfortable under its palm-frond awning, an ideal spot to perfect the art of *pumzika* – the Swahili word for snoozing.

The atoll itself is tiny – we could stroll around it in 20 minutes. But it is encircled by miles of virgin coral reefs, and at low tide the receding water exposes an infinity of lukewarm pools and wave-ribbed sands, where you feel you could walk forever and still not reach the horizon.

The tidelines were strewn with treasures of the deep: mottled cowries, strange starfish, and the pink satin carapaces of ghost crabs. Across the lagoon, a long, thin line of white marked where the waves were breaking on the outermost reefs. Beyond, sharp against the blue, were fishing dhows, whose shark's-fin sails have graced these waters since the time of Sinbad. And behind them nothing but a toppling wall of storm clouds coming down the coast with the warm *kaskazi* trade wind.

When the heat became too much to bear, we cooled off with goggles and flippers, slipping into the water where shoals of fish were circling the house reef just off the beach, rising and falling among the corals in a slow-motion ballet. Exquisite butterfly fish – their lips permanently pursed as if about to blow a kiss – glided past in stately golden convoys. Every species was a miracle of colour and design: angelfish with humbug stripes, Moorish idols like crescent moons, and parrotfish browsing on the corals with an audible crunch.

Everywhere at Mnemba, above and below the surface, there was life. At night, green turtles hauled themselves ashore to lay their eggs in the sand. One morning, immersed in a book, I looked up to see a suni, a tiny antelope no bigger than a hare, staring at me across my veranda.

By now, Mnemba had us hooked. Almost against my will, I could feel its insidious lethargy taking hold. Not for me the activities on offer: diving, kayaking, deep-sea angling. Instead, with Annabelle, we lolled and strolled, and the white band where I had worn my discarded wristwatch became as brown as the rest of me.

Lying in bed at night I could hear the dull roar of the ocean breaking on the reefs as the waves ran before the *kaskazi*, and from much closer came the wash of wavelets as they collapsed on the beach and fell back with a sigh, like the untroubled breathing of a sleeper. A few more days of this, I decided, and I could end up in thrall to the barefoot beach life for ever.

CHAPTER
TWENTY-FOUR

IT was now nearly five years since we had gone whale watching with Swanny in the Hebrides, and we had not forgotten his invitation to visit him in Mexico. So, in March 2004, having spoken to him again and then obtained a commission from the *Daily Telegraph*, we swapped the frosted fields of home for a nine-day cruise in the Baja's blissful desert climate.

Two days later we were idling in an oily calm across the Bay of La Paz. To the west lay the coast of Baja California, its rust-red rimrocks glowing in the early morning light. There was no wind, and in the ensuing silence when the engines were switched off, we could hear the breathing of the great whales all around us. First the hollow rush of expelled air from their cavernous lungs, then the deep intake of breath before the next deep dive.

When they blew, sending columns of moisture 30 feet into the sky, the spray drifted over us, smelling faintly of cabbage, and when they surfaced to peer at us with myopic eyes, it was impossible not to feel one's senses reaching out to them. Here we were, two species from alien worlds, drawn together by mutual curiosity; and who, watching them come so trustingly close, could fail to be moved, knowing how cruelly we had persecuted these innocent beasts down the centuries?

So quiet is the Baja, so empty and utterly unexpected, that you cannot believe Los Angeles and its teeming freeways are less than two hours away by air. Steinbeck wrote about it and perhaps Hemingway should have done. Otherwise, it has managed to remain off the map. The Baja itself is longer than Italy, a waterless peninsula hanging off the end of California with its tail in the Tropic of Cancer. Once you leave Tijuana you need a four-wheel drive to get anywhere. Or a boat.

The *Jacana*, our live-aboard home in this Mexican dreamland, was a 45-foot catamaran Swanny had chartered for the season. She had four comfortable cabins and a spacious galley-cum-dining saloon in which Anne, Swanny's sister, conjured up delicious feasts of char-grilled fish and enchiladas; and behind us we towed a *panga*, a fast fibreglass launch of the kind used by the local fishermen.

That night we anchored at Espíritu Santo, in an emerald cove rimmed by white shell sand, encircled by a Wild West landscape of red rimrocks and cactus forest. Next morning, woken at dawn by the rattle of the anchor chain, I surfaced for a cup of tea to find we were already under way, with Swanny sitting barefoot at the wheel.

'Today,' he announced, 'we are looking for Moby.' He meant the sperm whale, the biggest of the toothed whales, which can grow up to 60 feet long. 'They are usually quite shy,' he said, but he found one for us in half an hour, easily identified by its huge blunt head and the way it lolled on the surface. When it dived, sliding back into its own weightless world of indigo currents and sonic visions, Swanny switched on the hydrophone and we listened spellbound to the barrage of clicks the whale emitted as it hunted for squid in the sunless deeps.

We moved on. Swanny was desperate to show us a blue whale; but in the end the blue whale found us. We were floating far out in the bay, enjoying a picnic lunch on deck when we heard the familiar sound of a whale blowing and saw the animal heading straight towards us. It was unbelievably huge, like a Polaris submarine. Twice it circled us, no more than a boat's length away, and then it dived, passing directly beneath us. One flip of its tail could have sent us all to kingdom come; but there was no hint of menace in its unhurried movements as we high-fived each other in delight.

In the days that followed we saw nine more blue whales, 79 fin whales, 66 humpbacks, 13 Bryde's whales, two sei whales and another couple of sperm whales. Like Swanny, we had become adept at spotting the distant puffs of drifting spray, the sunlight gleaming on polished obsidian backs and the white shell-bursts of breaching humpbacks.

Yet even these encounters were upstaged by our meetings with the dolphins. Elsewhere I had seen maybe 30 at a time, but in the Sea of Cortez they turn up in their thousands, and by the time we flew home we had seen at least 23,000 common and bottlenose dolphins.

Joyfully, they raced towards us, determined to hitch a ride in our wake, and within minutes we were engulfed by a wall of spray and rolling bodies. They were chasing fish as they charged along, and they were not alone. All around us, boobies and pelicans were diving into the water. It was a feeding frenzy, and we were at the heart of it with thousands of dolphins strung out for a mile on either side.

Then, as suddenly as they had materialised out of the heat haze, they tired of their sport and peeled away to resume their wild hunt elsewhere, receding into the distance with a sound like breaking surf.

Never was life sweeter. By now, no longer pale-faced refugees from the English winter, we had kicked off our shoes and become ocean-going nomads like Swanny. At anchor we snorkelled among shoals of tropical fish or went beachcombing for cowries along sugar-white beaches with no footprints on them except those of wandering coyotes. At breakfast we gorged ourselves on fresh pineapples; and in the evenings, as the islands turned red and gold in the dying light, we drank margaritas and watched the moon come up over the Sierra de la Giganta.

No wonder Swanny called it the 'Sea of Dreams'. Sometimes, peering down into its turquoise depths, we spotted squadrons of mobula rays cruising past like stealth bombers on a mission. And one memorable morning Annabelle went swimming with the friendly sea lions of Isla Partida, whose doe-eyed youngsters were so inquisitive that they peered into her face mask from just inches away.

Too soon our voyage was nearly over, and we could not bear the thought of leaving.

But one special moment was still to come. It happened on our last night when we had set out to look for whales by moonlight. We jumped into the *panga* and raced out into the bay, leaving a fiery trail of bioluminescence in our wake.

Our luck was in. The moon was full, the sea was as smooth as glass and I began to understand why Swanny sometimes referred to it as 'the Silky'. He killed the engine, and in the silence of the moonglow we sat and listened to the deep sighs of spouting whales. There must have been at least a score – fin whales, Bryde's and humpbacks – all leisurely circling around us in the black-and-silver water.

Away to the southwest I could see the lights of La Paz, a reminder of the other universe from which we had come. But now and for a while yet, we remained in the company of the great leviathans, at peace with them and ourselves in Mexico's magical Sea of Dreams.

****

Afterwards, back home in Dorset again, it was hard to escape from the spell cast over us by the Baja. Of all the places I had ever seen, this was at the very forefront, but it was Swanny's presence that had made it so special for both of us.

No-one who has spent that much time with him can remain immune to his charm and boundless enthusiasm, and among the many distinguished individuals I have met in my career there are few I admire more.

Mexico was not the only trip we made together that year. In May we went walking in Aquitaine, following the course of the Aveyron as it wound its way past the medieval bastides of midmost France into the limestone country of the Causses with its delicate spider orchids and flurries of black-veined white butterflies – a species not seen in Britain for decades.

As the days warmed up, grasshoppers gave the heat a voice, a mindless shrilling that rose in waves from the ripening meadows between the limestone walls. No wonder we fought the Hundred Years' War to hang on to these indolent lands of lost content, great chunks of which have scarcely changed since the time of the Black Prince.

Most of the time we hardly saw a soul; but on the high road to Villefranche we met a shepherd sitting under a walnut tree. He was 65, he said, fingering his beret with tobacco-stained fingers, though he looked much older. I remarked on the beauty of the Causses. '*Oui*, but it is hard country,' he said. 'The soil is too thin. We have a little of everything: wine, cheese, fish, walnuts; but it is not a rich land.'

Two months later we were off on our travels again, this time to the Matobo Hills in Zimbabwe, where Cecil Rhodes, the founder of Rhodesia, is buried. His grave lies on the roof of a tumbledown landscape that was cast in granite 2,000 million years ago. In every direction, weather-stained pinnacles and rock castles stretch to the horizon, creating what the Ndebele people call Malindidzumu – the Place of Spirits.

Many of these extraordinary hills are nothing but colossal whalebacks. Others resemble the ruins of lost cities, with boulders balanced precariously on top of one another, like children's bricks. One shove, you feel, could send the whole lot crashing, and the best of it, with its sacred caves and prehistoric rock paintings, its black eagles and wandering leopards, is now a national park.

There, Ian MacDonald, who had known the park all his life, took us high into the hills to see a great hollow in the side of a cliff, like one half of an inverted dome which had been transformed by the paintings of the long-vanished San bushmen into a Sistine Chapel of Stone Age art, its walls covered with the outlines of matchstick men with bows and arrows pursuing giraffe, zebra, kudu and eland, each one as vivid as the day it was painted.

By the time we got back to the Matobo Hills Lodge the African sky was bedecked with stars. By pure coincidence we had arrived on the night when the planet Jupiter was about to be struck by a giant comet, offering the first opportunity the world had known to observe an extraterrestrial collision as it happened.

When the predicted time approached, we lay on our backs on the bare granite summit and stared up into deep space through our binoculars. There was Jupiter, bigger than the surrounding stars, and the air was so clear that for the first time in my life I could even see its moons. Was it my imagination or did the planet really glow brighter when the comet struck? In truth, I cannot say. What I do know is that, with uncanny precision, at the very moment of impact all the jackals of the Matobos began to cry, their keening voices rising and falling in the cold night air.

****

On our return from Zimbabwe our efforts to sell the cottage and buy Spick Hatch were still no further forward. It was a nail-biting time of intense frustration, even though the Taylors had kindly allowed Annabelle to keep her horse and donkey on their fields, so at least we felt we had one foot in the door – even if it was shod!

Then, nearly nine months later in March 2004, everything happened at once.

We went through all the legal formalities, exchanged contracts, and I walked around the cottage for the last time. I thought I would miss it, but as soon as its echoing rooms were empty the spell was broken, and Spick Hatch was ours. Only afterwards, so thrilled were we by our new home and its location, that I realised we had never even been upstairs to look at the bedrooms.

If ever a house was meant to be ours, Spick Hatch was the one. Honey-coloured and half-smothered in wisteria, it had everything I had ever dreamed of. Its long, low rooms were cool in summer and easy to keep warm in winter. At one end was a kitchen with a royal blue Aga oil-fired stove; at the other end – the oldest part of the house dating back a couple of centuries – was a giant inglenook fireplace under a massive oak lintel. Most important of all, the house faced south, its sunroom and windows framing glorious views of West Dorset's rolling hilltops, with no other building in sight except a solitary thatched cottage at the bottom of the valley, like something out of a Hardy novel.

Outside was a greenhouse, a garage, and a woodshed in which swallows nested, as well as a stone outhouse with a pantile roof, where we stored our garden tools.

The garden, enclosed on two sides by a clipped beech hedge, had everything I had ever dreamed of and more besides: a vegetable patch with an asparagus bed and a fruit cage; two walnut trees, magnolias, lawns and rose trellises, a goldfish pond, a rockery bright with alpine flowers – even a palm tree whose leathery leaves cracked and flapped in the breeze above a well at the head of a water garden.

Nor was that all. Beyond the orchard lay the home paddock and its stable, in which Annabelle's horse and donkey now lived, with a beech spinney at the end of it to provide us with an endless supply of firewood. At the southern end of the paddock stood a footbridge leading to another small meadow on the far side of the stream. And to our surprise, it seemed we were now also owners of West Milton weir, whose rushing waters provided a constant soundtrack throughout the year.

Our only regret was that none of our parents had lived to see our new home. How astounded my mother and father would have been at our purchase, and how incredibly proud, considering how far I had come from their inner-city roots in Edwardian London.

Finally, there were two other reasons why Spick Hatch was such a perfect fit. From the east end of the garden, I could look up the valley and still see the great prow of Eggardon Hill filling the skyline as it had done ever since I first came to live in Dorset; and only one field's length away on the other side of the stream stood Milton Mill, where Kenneth Allsop and I had shared such special times together, which made our move feel like the completion of a circle, as if meant to be.

To our delight we discovered that Spick Hatch itself was a natural haven for the wild plants and creatures that found refuge in our little valley. Lesser horseshoe bats – a Red List species as rare as the panda – roosted in our woodshed roof. Grass snakes lay coiled in our compost heaps and slow-worms hid in the rockery. Badgers turned up most nights to dig holes in the lawn as they searched for worms. Shy roe deer emerged from the woods at dawn to browse in the fields behind the house. Sea trout swam upstream to spawn in the pools at the bottom of our orchard. Kingfishers were a regular sight, and from time to time we would find the oily spraints and unmistakable five-toed tracks left overnight by a wandering otter.

Nor was our connection to the natural world confined to local wildlife alone. Our weathervane bore the bold silhouette of an elephant with trunk upraised, proclaiming to all passers-by that whoever lived at Spick Hatch was inextricably linked to wild Africa.

In February, snowdrops lay in deep drifts along the riverbanks, to be followed in spring by bluebells and ramsons. In April, the swallows returned to nest in the stable when our damp meadows were bright with cuckoo flowers. Wild daffodils appeared in the surrounding lanes, and as the year advanced, exquisite demoiselle flies fluttered over the water garden on wings of bronze that glittered like gauze in the bright May sunshine, while peacocks and red admiral butterflies clustered on our buddleia bushes, just as they had done in my childhood summers of long ago. Only the voice of the cuckoo was missing.

Houses, like people, often have their own personality, and Spick Hatch is no exception. Everyone who comes to visit us remarks on its serene and welcoming atmosphere. As for its situation, we could have wished for no finer accolade than that offered by Dick

Girling's wife, Caroline McGhie, then the *Daily Telegraph's* property correspondent. 'In terms of pure location,' she declared, 'it is one of the three best properties I have ever seen.'

Over the years, we have added a few extra touches to the house but have spent most of our time embellishing the garden. In the water garden, where a small stream bubbled straight out of the aquifer, we channelled it so that it issued from the mouth of a lion, carved in Hamstone by our friend Eva Harvey. Its course down to the orchard has also been greatly improved. It is now contained by stone walls overhung with ferns and gunnera and yellow flag iris; and in time the walls themselves have become smothered by green cushions of water-loving moss given to us by the novelist John Fowles, who lived in Lyme Regis and was a friend of Kenneth Allsop.

Beyond the stable we built a chicken run and bought a dozen hens to provide us with a regular supply of eggs. The stable itself acquired a new resident after Fudge the cob died, leaving Comfy, her donkey companion, alone and distraught, until Annabelle found a gentle skewbald mare called Maggie. Not long afterwards Comfy died, too, and was replaced by another young donkey from Devon. We called him Punda – the Swahili word for donkey – and he and Maggie soon became as inseparable.

It was around this time that my daughter Imogen moved back to Dorset. In the year 2000 she had married Lance, a likeable young Bristolian who she had met while working for Eurocamp in Denmark. Since then, they had been living in Yate, between Bristol and the Cotswolds, and were now the parents of two children. Luca, their daughter, was a lovable blonde five-year-old who reminded me of her mother when she was that age, and Jude, who was just a toddler, having followed two years later.

Sadly, within a few months of settling in, their marriage hit a rocky patch and they decided to separate. Lance remained in the family home and became the children's main carer, and it was at this point that we stepped in. To help Lance keep his job we helped as best we could, doing school runs and childminding. This meant the children spent a lot of time at Spick Hatch, feeding the animals, bringing their school friends back to play and organising treats and birthday parties.

Although this was a traumatic time for Luca and Jude it was a dream come true for Annabelle who, not having had children, delighted in caring for them as if they had been her own. During their school holidays we introduced them to Aldeburgh, and for me it was a special joy to take them to Cornwall and go surfing on Polzeath beach, as I had done so many years ago at their age.

Meanwhile, the travel assignments continued apace, and I found myself increasingly writing for the *Daily Telegraph*, whose travel editor, Graham Boynton, was a Zimbabwean who shared my passion for the African bush.

I knew now that I could never live anywhere else but in our little Dorset valley; yet whenever I watched the swallows departing at the end of summer, my heart went with them and I missed Africa with an unbearable longing. Hardly a day passed by without me thinking about the Luangwa River winding in immense silver coils through the Zambian bush or wondering if it was raining in the Serengeti.

Having been so many times I found it all too easy to conjure up images from previous safaris. A sleeping leopard recumbent in a fig tree, all golden sunlight and dappled shadow. A cheetah with burning amber eyes crouching atop a termite mound. A pride of lions with bloody jowls padding through the dew-soaked grass in line astern after a night's hunting on the plains.

I missed the ineluctable smell of Africa. The sun-dried hay meadow scent of the open savannah. The prickly odour of wild sage crushed underfoot. The stable-yard whiff of elephants and the glorious smell of dust freshly slaked when the first fat spots of rain begin to fall.

And how I missed the sounds of Africa. The urgent yelping of zebra stallions calling to their mares. The white-browed robin chats that greet the dawn and the red-chested cuckoos crying 'It-will-rain, it-will-rain' as thunder rolls across the plains. Together with the rumble of lions, the night-time sounds of frogs and scops owls and the cheerful music of Swahili voices, they created an African soundtrack that held me spellbound.

'All I wanted was to get back to Africa,' wrote Hemingway. 'We had not left it yet, but when I would awake in the night I would lie, listening, homesick for it already.'

Even so, not all our journeys were to Africa. For a long time, I had wanted Annabelle to meet Sir John Lister-Kaye, one of Scotland's most distinguished naturalists and a successful author with a string of bestsellers to his name. Born in 1946, he seemed destined for a life in industry until the 1960s, when fate took him down a different path to work in the Isle of Skye with Gavin Maxwell, the author of *Ring of Bright Water*, and his wild otters.

When Maxwell died in 1969 Lister-Kaye struck out on his own as an ecotourism pioneer, taking visitors into the hills and glens of Inverness-shire. The enterprise prospered and in 1977 he bought the House of Aigas, a rambling Victorian sporting lodge overlooking the Beauly River, complete with Gothic turrets and a great hall filled with ancestral portraits and enough antlers to re-equip an entire herd of red deer.

I had gone there soon afterwards in the dead of winter to be met by John, dressed like an old-time ghillie in tweeds, plus fours and a battered deerstalker. Together we watched whooper swans flying in at first light and heard their bugling voices echoing down the glens. In the River Glass he showed me my first otter, and later, unforgettably, climbed with me to the summit of Tom a' Chòinich – 'the hill of the moss' – with snow buntings drifting away from beneath our feet and tremendous views spread out before us, to Mam Soul and the Five Sisters of Kintail. After that it was impossible not to become friends.

Now, in the early spring of 2007, it was time for Annabelle to meet this gifted man and Lady Lucy, his wife. With John at the wheel, we parked in a glen where a shallow river ran. A row of alders grew on its banks, as old and gnarled as a grove of Greek olives, but this was no idyllic Aegean scene. A thousand feet above us the clouds were being torn to shreds in the cold spring sunshine, and there on a stick nest the size of an armchair sat a golden eagle.

Through my binoculars I could see it clearly. The hooked bill coloured slate and gold, and the frowning eyes as its head swivelled this way and that, keeping watch for its mate to return.

Of all the rare creatures that abound in Scotland, the golden eagle is the most sought after, the most iconic. Forget Landseer's portrait of a wild reg stag. This is the true monarch of the glen – a bird of prey with a seven-foot wingspan. At full stretch, dark pinions raking the air, it looks like a flying door; but its domain is vast. To see one – unless it is a mere speck in the sky – requires local expertise, and that is why we had come to Aigas to enlist John's aid.

By now, 30 years since he first arrived, Aigas had become a hugely successful field studies centre attracting visitors from all over the world. In just one week, without leaving his own 600 acres of wooded hillside, John or his enthusiastic team of rangers could show them ospreys, peregrines, badgers, and pine martens, and at Loch Cuil na Caillich in the heart of the estate, you could sit in a hide and watch the first European beavers to live wild in Scotland for 450 years.

During our stay, John had arranged a little expedition to the Isle of Skye to watch sea eagles, a bird known in Gaelic as *Iolaire sùil na grèine* – 'the eagle with the sunlit eye'. Widespread in Victorian times, they were driven to extinction by sheep farmers, gamekeepers and egg collectors; and the last pair known to nest on Skye had disappeared in 1916.

Their return to Scotland in the 1970s had been a major conservation success story. Reintroduced from Norway to the island of Rhum, they had steadily multiplied until there were now nearly 40 pairs scattered among the islands and sea lochs of the West Highland coast.

On our way back from Skye to the mainland we stopped off at Eilean Bàn, the tiny island that lies under the Skye Bridge at Kyle of Lochalsh. Its Gaelic name means 'white island', and it was here that John had come at Gavin Maxwell's invitation to write the story of Teko, the last of the *Bright Water* otters. With poignant timing, Teko died only two weeks after Maxwell himself died, and it was John who had buried the otter on the island.

He collected the key and ushered us into the house in which Maxwell had spent his last years. It was now a museum, maintained by the Eilean Ban Trust with help from the Born Free Foundation, and the inside was just as Maxwell left it. Even the Laphroaig whisky he enjoyed still stood on his drinks table.

The sitting room was a flotsam of antlers, otter skulls, letters and trophies that collectively portrayed the life of this extraordinary man. On one wall hung one of the harpoons he used to hunt basking sharks for their liver oil. On another, Arab daggers, and on his desk, written in longhand, was the first page of *Ring of Bright Water* that begins: '*I sit in a pitch-pine panelled kitchen living room, with an otter asleep upon its back among the cushions on the sofa...*'.

Today, otters still hunt in the swirling tides of Eilean Bàn, but we did not see one. In fact, for all John's insider knowledge we had not found them anywhere. There remained one last chance – a quick dash to the Beauly Firth before our flight home.

We were up at first light and the sky was cloudless, the firth like a mirror. Downstream at Kessock where a bridge spans the water, I could hear Inverness coming slowly to life. In the other direction, 15 miles away loomed the mountains of Affric, still piebald with snow, and no other sound but the cry of gulls.

A heron was fishing at the water's edge. Farther off I could see a great northern diver, but of otters there was no sign until a sudden movement caught my eye. First there was one head and then there were three, breaking the surface in quick succession.

Then three sleek bodies dived one after the other, followed by three sinuous tapering tails.

'This is what you pay your money for,' whispered John, and for the next half an hour we watched transfixed as the trio – a mother and her two cubs – romped and roistered through the floating bladderwrack, catching eels the same length as themselves and chomping them up with their sharp white teeth.

No wonder Annabelle was moved to tears. What our binoculars captured that morning exceeded anything I had ever seen in a wildlife TV documentary. At one point the otters upset a pair of mute swans. The cob bore down on them, hissing furiously. But they blithely ignored him and went on fishing and play-fighting in the sharp spring light as the sun came over the hills behind us and the firth turned to burnished gold and silver.

CHAPTER
TWENTY-FIVE

HAVING happily settled down at Spick Hatch, I realised that for the first time in my life since the 1970s I was free to play football again. Powerstock had a village team that used to compete in a Sunday league and, after a few weeks of jogging to try and get fit, I joined their pre-season kickabouts. Eventually, wearing knee supports and elastic bandages around both ankles, I felt fit enough to turn out for the team, most of whom were several decades younger than me.

It was a salutary experience. Often, my mind would tell me where I needed to go, but my legs would not get me there; and sometimes, if I fell over after a heavy challenge, my teammates would rush up to see if I had died!

But there were also moments of pure joy that recalled my glory days with Wimbledon Juniors. Anyone who has played the game will know the feeling of delivering a perfectly weighted pass, of bringing the ball under control and then putting your foot through it, hitting it sweetly with all the laces and watching it end up in the back of the net.

The fact that I played as striker says a lot about the standard of Sunday league football; but the few goals I scored gave me as much pleasure as any I had claimed in the past. Of course, it could not last, and in 2008, after returning from a hernia operation at the age of 73, I decided to hang up my boots.

Annabelle, meanwhile, had signed on for a six-week course in beekeeping. It was the first one to be offered by the West Dorset Beekeepers' Association and resulted in the arrival that year of a hive with a colony of around 70,000 bees. Two years later we had three hives behind the chicken run, supporting a population of more than 200,000 bees, producing up to 150 pounds of honey in a good summer.

Every September we would return to Aldeburgh to spend a week with Annabelle's family, either renting a cottage in Thorpeness or staying with her brother Michael and Emma, his partner, on the edge of Minsmere. As I was away so often on travel-writing trips, these were usually our own true holidays.

The only exception was a week in May on Bryher in the Isles of Scilly. We had taken Michael and Emma there for the first time ten years ago and they had become as besotted with the islands as we were.

On one such visit we had planned an evening boat trip to watch the local crews participating in the annual World Pilot Gig Championships. No sooner had we seated ourselves in the bows than we spotted my ex-wife Sarah coming aboard with her new partner. Unbeknown to each other, both parties had booked into Bryher, never dreaming we might meet up.

After the initial moment of surprise and embarrassment, I introduced them to Michael and Emma, after which they sat themselves down at the other end of the boat. Moments later, once we were under way, Michael turned to me with a broad grin and said quietly: 'Brian, do you realise what this means? You are probably the only man anywhere in the Atlantic at this moment with two wives in the same boat.'

CHAPTER TWENTY-FIVE

****

In October 2012, a chance meeting on Exmoor resulted in a new addition to our family after I had gone there to write a piece for the *Daily Telegraph* on dark skies. Exmoor had just been designated as an International Dark Sky Reserve – the first place in Europe to receive this accolade, being one of the few corners of England where low levels of light pollution allow visitors to enjoy night skies that have long since disappeared elsewhere.

On Winsford Hill the darkness was absolute. There was no moon, no light of any kind except for the distant galaxy of the Welsh coast glittering with frosty brilliance on the eastern horizon, and a few remote farmsteads blinking like red dwarfs in the unseen combes below. Otherwise, Exmoor was one vast black hole of silence – the perfect venue for a spot of stargazing.

In Dulverton next morning the clear skies had vanished, and the Barle Valley with its salmon pools and hanging woods was gift-wrapped in fog. I had hoped to go looking for Exmoor's red stags, Britain's largest wild land mammals. October was a good time to see them on Exmoor when the hillsides echo to their bellowing – known as 'bolving' – but instead we were sidetracked by an altogether different animal.

With their mealy muzzles and small ears, Exmoor ponies are a hardy breed whose lineage goes back to Celtic times. In winter they eat gorse and heather and are so perfectly insulated against the cold that snow can settle on their backs without melting.

Out of interest we called in at the Exmoor Pony Centre at Dulverton, a charity-run business owned by the Moorland Mousie Trust, which is dedicated to promoting and protecting the last 350 ponies that still roam free across the national park. *Moorland Mousie* was the title of a popular children's book of the 1920s, and the Trust itself, founded in 1998, helps to find foster homes for young foals that cannot be accommodated on the Moor.

Ever since Maggie, our skewbald mare, had died the previous year, Annabelle had been desperate to find a replacement, and adopting an Exmoor foal seemed like the ideal solution.

So it was, in the spring of 2013, that a horsebox arrived at Spick Hatch and out stepped a perfect example of the breed. Since he was only 14 months old, and all our animals had Swahili names, we called him Toto (baby).

****

One of our most memorable adventures that year took place at Bear Cave Mountain Lodge in the Yukon, only a snowball's throw from the Arctic Circle. It stands on the banks of the Fishing Branch River and is only open for six weeks of the year in late autumn.

That is when 35,000 chum salmon run up the river to spawn. Fed by underground springs, its pure waters remain unfrozen all-year round, and the presence of so many fish attract grizzly bears – as many as 40 every season – that gather on its banks to pile on the pounds before hibernating in the limestone caverns that honeycomb Bear Cave.

As they wade through the river an extraordinary transformation takes place. Within minutes their wet fur freezes in the sub-zero temperatures and they become ice bears, with hoar frost glittering on their backs and icicles dangling from their bellies – and this was the image that had lured us halfway across the world to witness this unique spectacle in October 2013.

Set in an area the size of Switzerland with only 350 inhabitants, the lodge is unbelievably remote. To reach it we flew north from Vancouver to Dawson City, home of the 1898 Klondike Gold Rush, where the streets are still made of pay dirt and permafrost and the wooden buildings with their false fronts and boardwalks resemble a spaghetti western film set.

From here the only access to Bear Cave Mountain was a stunning two-hour helicopter ride across a far-reaching emptiness of deep-frozen rivers and boreal forests bounded by range upon range of chaste white mountains rolling north to the Beaufort Sea.

On we flew, across a roadless desolation of snow-covered tundra known only to the migrating caribou and the wolves that follow them, until at last we touched down on the stony shores of the Fishing Branch River to be greeted by Phil Timpany, who runs the lodge and Smoky, the Norwegian elkhound who was his only companion for much of the time.

Like so many trips, the ones that stand out most vividly are those that revolve around extraordinary individuals, and this was no exception. Timpany is the bear-whisperer of North Yukon. He is to grizzlies what George Adamson was to lions and does not even carry a can of pepper spray – the most popular bear deterrent. His weapon of last resort is a 12-gauge pump-action shotgun, but in all his 22 years at Bear Cave Mountain he had never had to use it.

On our first morning we grabbed a coffee and stepped out into the bone-clenching chill of a North Yukon dawn. The sky was clear, but sunup was still an hour away as we followed Timpany down to the river with Smoky at our heels.

Now the stage was set. Locked in an all-embracing silence, we sat on a log at the water's edge and waited for the first bears to arrive as ravens flitted through the trees like souls. The river flowed past us, swift and shallow, its gin-clear waters an angler's dream, alive with the outlines of spawning fish.

Some mornings, said Timpany in his John Wayne drawl, he saw moose by the riverside; caribou and wolverine, too; and at night when the aurora borealis swirled and flickered overhead he would hear the eerie harmonies of wolves in the spruce forests.

In his early years in grizzly country, he had worked as a guide for trophy hunters but tired of the bloodletting and got a job studying chum salmon before moving to Bear Cave Mountain in 1991. Since then, having spent more than 2,000 days in the company of grizzlies, he had come to know them better than anyone. His relationship with bears was based on mutual respect, demolishing the grizzly's fearsome reputation as a natural born killer. 'They are such forgiving animals,' he said. 'When you enter their world, you realise what a peaceful coexistence they enjoy.'

Even when no bears were in sight their spine-tingling presence was all-powerful; but we did not have to wait for long. Out of the mist hanging over the river emerged a dark apparition. It was the big male called Stanley, patrolling the riverbank with a rolling swagger as if all the world belonged to him. Eleven years old and just entering his prime, he was the spirit of winter made flesh and bone, resplendent in his ice-armoured coat.

Closer and closer he came until the bear was no more than three paces away from where we sat side by side on the iron-hard ground. 'Good to see you, Stanley,' said Timpany softly, as my heartbeat increased a notch or two. But North America's most fearsome predator ignored us completely. Clearly, he was not interested in snacking on a writer long past his sell-by date.

******

Over the next decade we continued to travel the world together. In the Caribbean we went cruising on board the *Star Clipper*, a four-masted staysail barquentine, lying spreadeagled in the widows' nets under the bowsprit as dolphins joyfully rode the waves beneath us; but most of my trips were set firmly within the realms of eco-tourism, searching for jaguars in the Pantanal or following in Jim Corbett's footsteps to track tigers in the foothills of the Himalayas. And always, Africa remained my first and foremost destination.

There, thanks to the financial benefits of ecotourism, a living elephant was now worth more than £1 million over its lifetime, and nowhere was this this truer than at Elephant Watch Camp in Samburu National Reserve. The Masai Mara may be Kenya's top tourist destination but its soul lies in the north, where the green highlands fall away into an arid wilderness the size of Britain and the proud Samburu people still follow their livestock herds across the surrounding rangelands.

Sharing their land are the beautiful dry-country animals that make Samburu special: reticulated giraffe, beisa oryx and Grevy's zebra – the world's most beautiful wild horse. But above all, Samburu is elephant country – hence the distinguished presence of Iain Douglas-Hamilton, the world authority on elephant behaviour, and the headquarters of Save the Elephants, the organisation he founded in 1993.

When I first met Iain and Oria, his glamorous Italian-born wife in 1974 they were already famous, having written *Among the Elephants*, an international bestseller which described their adventures while studying elephant behaviour in Tanzania's Lake

Manyara National Park. It was the last night of my first visit to Africa, and with typical Kenyan hospitality, although I was simply a young journalist they had never met before, they insisted on driving me to Nairobi airport for my flight home and we have remained friends ever since.

Elephant Watch Camp itself is set on the banks of the Ewaso Nyiro just a few miles upstream from Iain's office and was created by Oria in 2001. 'I built it with dead trees the elephants had knocked down,' she told me, 'and the spot I chose was the place our bulls loved to frequent. Gorbachev, Mungu, Kenyatta and Roosevelt – they were always there. No-one ever chased them away.'

Shaded by giant river acacias, the camp was exquisitely beautiful, a fusion of luxury bush living and Bedouin bohemia, entirely open to the comings and goings of the animal world. At breakfast time, eagle owls muttered to each other from the treetops. At night shy spotted genets with long, slender tails wandered among the dining tables.

When I returned there in 2015 it was Saba, Oria's eldest daughter, who had taken over as the glamorous chatelaine of Elephant Watch Camp and it was hard to think of anyone more suited to the task.

When she was just six weeks old her mother decided she should meet her first wild elephant, a matriarch called Virgo, one of the 400 animals her father was studying in Tanzania's Lake Manyara National Park. 'Although far too young to remember it I was told that when Virgo saw me, she stretched out her trunk and took a good long sniff to get my scent,' she said. 'Then she brought her own calf forward as if to introduce it to my mother.'

After university she worked with Save the Rhino Trust in Namibia before eventually joining Save the Elephants as her father's chief executive in 1997, and it was then, while working for STE, that she was talent-spotted by the BBC Natural History Unit and embarked on a career as a wildlife film-maker.

In 2006 she married Frank Pope, a former *Times* correspondent and marine archaeologist, and the couple now lived at Elephant Watch Camp with their three children.

Nowhere else in the world, I discovered, could you be on first-name terms with so many wild elephants. During her father's research it was necessary to get to know Samburu's elephants as individuals, since when 900 had been named and separated into their respected families.

Early next day we drove out to meet them. The morning sun fell like a blessing across the Samburu floodplains, pouring away towards the sacred mountain of Ololokwe in the blue distance beyond. 'There is an etiquette to approaching elephants,' said Saba. 'You never encroach on their space. Instead, you let them make the decisions and allow them to feel confident enough to ignore you. It is something I acquired from my father, learning how to read the nuances of animal behaviour, and then reacting appropriately.'

I hoped she was right because standing right in the path of our vehicle was a large bull elephant. 'That's Edison,' she said, and it was all too apparent that Edison was in musth, stoked up with testosterone and eager to mate. Elephant bulls can be unpredictable at this time, and I have seen what they are capable of.

In the visitor centre at Save the Elephants' headquarters is the trashed Land Cruiser in which two researchers nearly lost their lives. It happened in 2002 when they witnessed a battle between two bull elephants known as Abe Lincoln and Rommel. When Lincoln gained the upper hand, Rommel took out his frustration on the vehicle and flipped it over with his tusks.

That was the image that flickered through my mind as Saba switched off the ignition and Edison strode towards us, extending the tip of his trunk until it was hovering only inches from my forearm. Slowly he followed the outline of my body until I could feel his warm breath on the side of my face. Then, inexplicably, he brushed past and stood behind us with tusks and trunk laid at full length on our canvas roof.

Time stopped. In the silence, I could hear wood doves calling all around us. Then he was gone, a dark shadow drifting away through the trees. 'Well done,' said Saba afterwards. 'You passed the flinch test with flying colours.'

It was an unforgettable meeting, involving total trust between all three individuals involved – two humans and one elephant – and only if you stay at Elephant Watch Camp are such close encounters possible.

CHAPTER TWENTY-SIX

IN 2014 Bradt Travel Guides kindly published *Savannah Diaries*. Distilled from four decades of notes and press clippings, it was envisaged as a celebration of Africa's wildlife and wild places and the extraordinary individuals I had met there during my travels.

Somebody at *The Telegraph* asked me how many times I had been on safari. 'I got to a hundred and lost count,' was the answer, and I remember thinking what an incredible privilege it was and how lucky I had been, having visited all the parks and game reserves I used to dream about. The only glaring gaps were Uganda and Malawi, and Zakouma National Park in Chad.

Over the years I had covered so much ground in the Mara-Serengeti ecosystem that I knew it almost as intimately as Dorset; but there remained one favourite area that Annabelle and I had never explored together.

Back in the 1980s I was introduced to Baron Hugo van Lawick, one of the foremost wildlife film-makers of his day. For ten years, until they were divorced in 1974, he had been married to Jane Goodall, the primatologist renowned for her work in Tanzania with the chimpanzees of Gombe Stream.

When I met him, he was dividing his time between his London apartment in Hampstead and a luxurious camp known as 'Hugo's Hilton', situated just outside the southern end of the Serengeti National Park near Ndutu Safari Lodge.

In 1992 he was shooting a film called *Cheetahs: The Blood Brothers* – screened to great acclaim on ITV the following year. He had asked me to write the commentary script, and so I joined him at his camp for two unforgettable weeks in the Serengeti.

We got up every day before dawn to sneak into the park without having to pay entry fees and then drove eastwards across country to the Gol Kopjes, where the gazelles gathered in their thousands to browse on the short-grass plains. In turn their presence attracted the cheetahs that preyed on them, including the two brothers who featured in Hugo's film.

Here, drinking endless cups of coffee, Hugo and I would sit in his Land Rover, waiting for the golden hour, that magical time in Africa when the sun sinks towards the horizon, drenching the plains in amber light as the heat subsides and the gazelles awake to chase each other across the grass as if for the sheer joy of being alive.

This was also the prime time for filming the cheetahs as they emerged from the shade of the kopjes to hunt. Seen from afar, these brooding islands of granite boulders rise from the Serengeti's endless skylines like broken battleships turned to stone; and in the emptiness of the plains, they were the stars we steered by.

Afterwards, when the light had gone and Hugo had packed away his camera, we would drive back to camp in the dark for a welcome shower and a campfire supper.

After that safari, I returned several times to the Serengeti. Usually this involved a long and tiring driving from Arusha; but descending at last towards Olduvai there came a moment that never failed to lift my heart: the first glimpse of the plains, a sunlit ocean of grass and cloud shadows rolling away past the Gol Mountains to the ends of the earth.

For me, of all the world's wild places, the Serengeti is without equal. At upwards of 5,000 feet the light is dazzling. The air smells of dust and game and grasses that ripple for mile after mile in the dry highland wind with seldom a road and never a fence and nothing to break the distant skyline except for the lonely kopjes and the horned heads of the animals that lift their heads to stare at your approach.

Across this stage moved the annual migration, a million wildebeest and 200,000 zebras – the greatest wildlife spectacle on earth – pursued by the carnivores as the herds chased the rains from Tanzania to Kenya and back on their endless journey.

In his novel, *The Roots of Heaven*, Romain Gary saw the African elephant as a giant symbol of liberty; but for me the wildebeest migration is a far more potent metaphor. To watch that living mass of animals swarming over the eastern plains, to live under canvas in the sun and the wind, to fall asleep to their sonorous grunting and wake at dawn to the song of the lion is to know you are truly alive.

The memory of that open rolling country and the feeling of freedom it induced had stayed with me ever since, and in September 2019 I finally achieved my dream of returning there with Annabelle.

Lying up against the endless plains of the Loliondo Game Controlled Area, this part of the eastern Serengeti had long been renowned as a cheetah stronghold. For 20 years it was set aside exclusively for big-cat conservation and was consequently off limits to the public until a safari company, Asilia Africa, were given permission to build Namiri Plains Camp there in 2014. Since then, it had acquired an unrivalled reputation for sightings of the Serengeti's most sought-after predators, not only cheetahs but lions, leopards, servals, and caracals.

In just seven days we saw 20 cheetahs, more than 60 lions and, uniquely, a rare serval cat with a glossy black coat which had established its home range not far from camp.

The camp itself – the first to be built on the remote eastern plains – is unashamedly high-end; but Namiri's main attraction was the exceptional quality of its game-viewing. The nearest camp is at least an hour's drive away, meaning that when you come across the resident carnivores there is seldom another vehicle in sight.

Around the camp lay a classic Serengeti parkland of dappled glades and majestic acacias with their iconic flat-roofed canopies. But once we drove beyond the woodlands there was nothing but endless savannah in which fleets of kopjes drew the eye, measuring the yawning distance.

In every direction the land reached out to a horizon so wide and far away I could sense the curve of the earth as it rolled through space to meet the rising sun. These were the hunting grounds of the lions and cheetahs we had come to see; but in searching for them we found ourselves falling under the spell of the plains themselves. Their remoteness unwittingly takes hold of you, a kind of madness, like the beginning of a love affair, until you feel you could drive for ever and never want the days to end.

These eastern plains have a swell to them, like the rise and fall of a heavy sea, and beyond every wave lay some new delight: a pair of Kori bustards – the world's heaviest flying birds – or a golden jackal, its tail streaming out behind, trotting so lightly its feet hardly seemed to touch the earth.

For all their emptiness the plains are never silent. Our nights echoed to the rumble of lions whose cavernous groans could be heard five miles away before subsiding with a rhythmic coda of deep-throated grunts that never fail to thrill me to the core; and from dawn to dusk every hour was filled with the thin cries of larks and pipits, the demented shrieks of crowned lapwings and the shrill voices of zebra stallions calling to their mares.

A week or so ago there was not a zebra in sight, forcing the lions to stay alive by catching warthogs. But this was October. The seasons were changing, and the short rains had begun. In the late afternoons, great anvil-headed cloud castles arose, trailing dark curtains of rain across the plains. Wherever the showers touched the earth, a flush of green grass appeared. Morning glory flowers raised their pale pink trumpets to the sky, and swallows that had gathered on the telephone wires of home now hawked for insects above browsing herds of Grant's gazelles.

The rain washed the dust from the air, enhancing its diamond-bright clarity in which the blue faraway outlines of Ngorongoro and the Gol Mountains stood out sharply to the south, and in the wake of the rains the first zebras had come, moving down from their dry-season refuge in the Masai Mara.

From their vantage points on the kopjes, the lions of the Namiri Plains watched their arrival as they lay outlined on the rocks, manes rippling in the wind as they sensed their season of plenty was at hand.

We drove across a shallow valley in which five cheetahs rose out of the grass – a mother and her four subadult youngsters. Their slim bellies showed they had not yet eaten as they stared intently at a distant herd of gazelles, but we did not stop.

Instead, we continued our journey across the Namiri pride lands until we came to a lonely kopje where an old male lion lay fast asleep on a whale-backed rock. As we drove closer it was clear he had been in the wars. His body was a map of scars. His haunches were still bleeding from a recent battle, and he lay with his head on one side, slack-jawed and panting in the heat as if weighed down by the weight of years.

Patena, our keen-eyed Maasai guide, pulled out his camera and began to check his previous photos. 'Wow!' he exclaimed. 'It's Ziggy.'

When Namiri Plains Camp opened in 2014 the local prides were dominated by a magnificent pair of male lions. One sported a luxuriant mane of black dreadlocks, for which he became known as Bob (after the reggae music star, Bob Marley); and his blond-maned companion was named Ziggy, after Marley's son.

Together they had reigned unchallenged across the plains until driven out by a powerful coalition of six nomadic males, after which Bob had died and nobody knew what had happened to Ziggy – until we found him.

Watching that grizzled old warrior with his blunt canines and weary eyes, I thought of the cubs he had fathered and the battles he had won, sharing his glory days with Bob at his side. Fourteen times in his life he would have witnessed the arrival of the great migration when the plains were black with wildebeest. Now his race was almost run. Banished to this lonely spot, he had been forced to survive like a fugitive, scavenging scraps from the kills of others as his strength ebbed away. But for a while yet, having been born around 15 years ago, he was still the oldest male lion in the Serengeti.

Afterwards, back home again in Dorset, I could not forget the sight of him, hauling himself slowly to his feet to lap rainwater from a puddle at the foot of the rocks. It was yet another of those milestone moments that measured the course of my life, as poignant in its own way as when I had crossed the Pyrenees for my 50th birthday, and when, in the softly fading light of a Suffolk spring evening, I had first seen the girl I would marry.

What a long road it had been, from Surrey in wartime to the Serengeti. I was now 84 and the sand in the hourglass was running out. How many more times, I wondered, would I watch the wildebeest flooding across the savannah as Ziggy had done? And for how much longer would lions continue to walk through my life and my dreams?

EPILOGUE

'One day not far off, perhaps, the last lion will roar his challenge over Musiara Marsh to the boundless plains beyond, to be followed by a silence that will last through eternity.'

From *The Marsh Lions* (Bradt, 2012)

AFTER spending a quiet Christmas at home, Annabelle and I set off for Africa again in January 2020. This time we were guiding a group of friends and neighbours around Kenya's Masai Mara wildlife conservancies.

It was always good to be back in the Mara, despite the unseasonal rains which made game-driving difficult at times. But the conservancies never fail to deliver, and we enjoyed daily encounters with leopards and lion prides and watched the rare spectacle of three subadult cheetahs trying to catch an aardwolf, which eventually managed to evade its pursuers by diving down an old warthog burrow.

It was not until we returned home at the end of January that we heard of the deadly coronavirus outbreak, first identified in December in Wuhan, a Chinese city of more than 11 million people. It was thought to have started in the Huanan seafood market, which also sold various wildlife species as well as fish, leading to conjecture that it originally came from bats but had jumped the species barrier, possibly using pangolins – the world's most illegally traded mammal – as a bridge before infecting humans.

Once the genie was out of the bottle the virus spread quickly. By the end of January, the World Health Organisation had declared the outbreak a 'Public Health Emergency of International Concern'. On 11th March it was upgraded to a Global Pandemic, and by the time I had celebrated my 85th birthday in April, it had spread to 200 countries, infecting more than three million people, resulting in 217,000 deaths.

In the USA alone it had killed more Americans than all those who lost their lives in the Vietnam War, resulting in the biggest global recession since the Great Depression.

Among the biggest economic casualties was the tourist business. Almost overnight, planes were grounded, and the trade collapsed, with disastrous consequences for ecotourism and the wildlife whose survival it sustained.

Nowhere is this truer than in Africa. When I became a travel writer in the 1970s, safaris were the realm of the seriously rich and revolved mostly around trophy hunting. But all over the world, what later became known as ecotourism was taking root and Africa was at the forefront.

When the decade began, the entire continent was still locked in an age of innocence. Wildlife was abundant in numbers that seem scarcely credible today, and tourism was in its infancy. Even in 1982 there were fewer than a dozen camps and lodges in Kenya's Masai Mara national reserve.

All over Africa, though, change was in the wind and high-end tourism was on the march. From Ngorongoro to the Okavango Delta, I watched as new camps and lodges sprang up almost overnight. Gone were the old long-drop lavatories and bush bucket showers dangling from a tree. In their place came canvas suites the size of tithe barns with teak decks and private plunge pools.

Back then, when the lodges started changing, I remember sitting around the fire at Jack's Camp in Botswana, listening to Ralph Bousfield, its enigmatic owner, telling me how the old-time trophy-hunting safaris that had sustained his father were now in full retreat. Photography safaris were what people wanted now, he said, and the luxury of boundless space which Africa had in abundance, underlining the growing acceptance of ecotourism and its vital role in underpinning the economic viability of Africa's last wild strongholds.

According to the Sheldrick Wildlife Trust, a living elephant is now worth more than $1.6 million over its lifetime, largely because of its value to ecotourism, and the same can be said of lions, an endangered species whose mere presence in Kenya is worth at least $1 billion every year. No wonder Richard Leakey called them: 'Kenya's unpaid workers, operating round the clock to boost the country's vital tourist industry.'

In 2019, according to the World Travel and Tourism Council, wildlife tourism in Africa employed 3.6 million people and was worth $29.3 billion. Now, however, its future looks bleak. Following the lockdown on international travel, camps and safari lodges closed in droves, leaving Africa's iconic wildlife under threat and leading to fears that it could lead to a vast increase in poaching for the bushmeat trade. With no source of income, some will feel forced to kill animals just to stay alive, while others may poach to make money.

How lucky I was to see it all when the going was good. If I were to add up all the days of my life spent on safari, they would amount to at least three years under canvas in the bush – much of it in the company of wild Africa's most distinguished individuals.

Somehow, miraculously, the priceless parks and game reserves have managed to remain inviolate, showcasing the natural world at its most sublime. The Serengeti wildebeest are still embarking on their great annual migration. Somewhere in the vastness of the savannah, cheetahs will be sitting on top of a termite mound, surveying the plains with amber eyes, and across Africa, from Kenya to the Great Karoo, the roar of the lion still greets the dawn - but for how much longer?

How unforgivable it would be to lose it all on our watch. That is the pain I find hardest to bear: having seen ecotourism grow from its first green shoots, and encouraged its spread throughout my entire journalistic career, only to see it collapse, leaving wildlife and wild places at risk all over the world, together with the livelihoods of all those who rely on it for their own survival.

For now, any hopes of returning to Africa or even crossing the Tamar are clouded by uncertainty. Yet when the coronavirus first arrived in Britain it brought about a profound change in the countryside. It was impossible not to be aware of it – the return of an ancient silence, the like of which I had not experienced since I first came to Dorset half a century ago.

The all-enveloping hush imposed by the nationwide policy of self-isolation magnified all the sounds of the natural world quietly going about its business, untouched by the catastrophe that has turned our own world upside down. Was it my imagination or was the dawn chorus louder than ever? Blackbirds, thrushes, deep-throated wood pigeons – all joined in – singing a song of hope and reassurance that nature is carrying on regardless.

The air was so much cleaner, too; a joy to breathe. And I swear I could smell the tang of the Atlantic and its forbidden beaches, even though they are a hundred miles away.

By day, the sky was a vault of blue unsullied by the contrails of the grounded jet liners, and at night the stars were the brightest I had seen since I was in the Kalahari twenty years ago. The bushmen of Botswana, who believe the stars to be hunters in the heavens, say they can hear them in the profound stillness of the desert. But all I could hear were the quavering voices of tawny owls in the woods behind Milton Mill.

That was the silver lining to the current pandemic; the simple pleasures that manifested themselves in pursuing a lockdown life at home: planting potatoes, watching the first orange-tip butterflies emerge and seeing the first swallows return, joyfully swooping over the meadows as if to confirm that for us, too, the world will one day return to normal.

Brian Jackman, West Milton, April 2020

ACKNOWLEDGEMENTS

THE journeys featured in this book span my lifetime in journalism, from the 1970s to the present day. Among them are extracts from articles written for the *Sunday Times* on Jerez, George Adamson, Mike Tomkies, the Pyrenees, Tarka the Otter, Tsavo's bloody ivory, the Isles of Scilly, East Germany, Namibia, and Mnemba Atoll in Zanzibar. Permission to use these was kindly granted courtesy of the *Sunday Times*/News Licensing.

I am equally grateful to the *Daily Telegraph* for generously allowing me to reproduce extracts from pieces I have written for their travel pages over the years, and to Little Toller Books for allowing me to include my tribute to Kenneth Allsop, which appeared as the foreword in their 2011 edition of *In the Country*.

As for the lines from 'Bloody Orkney' quoted in chapter 10, they are attributed to a poem written by a sailor, Captain Hamish Blair, in 1952 – the year before my visit to the islands as an ordinary seaman under training during my national service in the Royal Navy – while those quoted in chapter 19 come from *The Ballad of the Royal Ann* in a section called 'The Reefs' by the Cornish poet and novelist Crosbie Garstin, published by William Heinemann in 1922. The lyrics from 'Streamline Train' at the beginning of Part One were written by the late American blues singer, Red Nelson, in 1936.

At the *Sunday Times* I would particularly like to pay homage to the late Sir Harold Evans, surely Fleet Street's greatest editor, for taking me on in the first place, and to single out Ian Jack and Richard Girling, whose subediting skills not only transmuted the base metal of my copy but also honed my raw talent as a wordsmith in the process. At the *Daily Telegraph*, I would like to extend my gratitude to an illustrious line of travel editors, from Gill Charlton and Graham Boynton to Charlie Starmer-Smith, Michael Kerr and Joanna Symons, and above all to Andrew Purvis for his unstinting support over the years.

During my travels I met so many extraordinary and gifted people from all walks of life who gave so generously of their time and allowed me into their private worlds. Some – Hugh Miles, Christopher Swann, Roger Lovegrove and Sir John Lister-Kaye – have since become the best of friends; and the same holds true for many of those I met on safari in Africa, a long list including Jonathan Scott, Tony Fitzjohn, David Coulson, Virginia McKenna, Ron and Pauline Beaton and the Douglas-Hamilton family, all of whom have enriched my life through the adventures we shared.

Writing this memoir has been like living those days all over again, and my only concern has been for all my dear friends who have not found their way into the narrative. If you are one of them, I apologise with all my heart and would like to say that just because they are not mentioned does not mean I do not love you or think of you often.

As for the book itself, nothing could have been accomplished without the tireless efforts of Jonny Pegg, my literary agent. I would also like to extend my heartfelt thanks to Adrian Phillips at Bradt for his faith in the project, and the unerring eagle eye of Rachel Fielding, my editor.

Finally, as ever, my eternal thanks to Annabelle, my inspirational wife and constant travelling companion, who never questioned my long hours in front of the computer screen and whose passion for wildlife and wild places sometimes even surpasses my own.

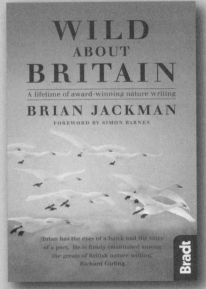

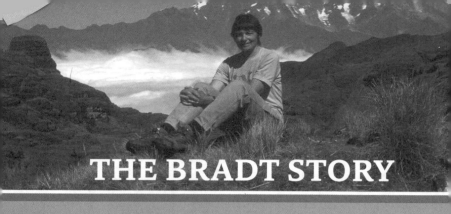

THE BRADT STORY

In the beginning

It all began in 1974 on an Amazon river barge. During an 18-month trip through South America, two adventurous young backpackers – Hilary Bradt and her then husband, George – decided to write about the hiking trails they had discovered through the Andes. *Backpacking Along Ancient Ways in Peru and Bolivia* included the very first descriptions of the Inca Trail. It was the start of a colourful journey to becoming one of the best-loved travel publishers in the world; you can read the full story on our website (www. bradtguides.com/ourstory).

Getting there first

Hilary quickly gained a reputation for being a true travel pioneer, and in the 1980s she started to focus on guides to places overlooked by other publishers. The Bradt Guides list became a roll call of guidebook 'firsts'. We published the first guide to Madagascar, followed by Mauritius, Czechoslovakia and Vietnam. The 1990s saw the beginning of our extensive coverage of Africa: Tanzania, Uganda, South Africa, and Eritrea. Later, post-conflict guides became a feature: Rwanda, Mozambique, Angola, Sierra Leone, Bosnia and Kosovo.

Comprehensive – and with a conscience

Today, we are the world's largest independently owned travel publisher, with more than 200 titles, from full-cour and wildlife guides to Slow Travel guides like this one. However, our ethos remain unchanged. Hilary is still keenly involved and we still get there first: two-thirds of Bradt guides have no direct competition.

But we don't just get there first. Our guides are also known for being more comprehensive than any other series. We avoid templates and tick-lists. Each guide is a one-of-a-kind expression of a expert author's interests, knowledge and enthusiasm for telling it how it really is.

And a commitment to wildlife, conservation and respect for local communities has always been at the heart of our books. Bradt Guides was championing sustainable travel before a other guidebook publisher.

Thank you!

We can only do what we do because of the support of readers like you – people who value less-obvious experiences, less-visited places and a more thoughtfu approach to travel. Those who, like us, t travel seriously.

Bradt GUIDES
TRAVEL TAKEN SERIOUSLY